# Life in
# Medieval
# Ireland

ANGLO—NORMAN
IRELAND
c.1330

O'Neills

Carrickfergus

Earldom
of Ulster
(de Burgh)

Dundalk

Lordship
of Connacht
(de Burgh)

Drogheda

River Shannon

Galway

Dublin

Earldom
of Kildare
(Fitzgerald)

Kilkenny

River Barrow

Limerick

Wexford

New Ross

Earldom
of Desmond
(Fitzgerald)

Cork

● Town
∧∧ Wicklow Mountains

# LIFE IN MEDIEVAL IRELAND

## WITCHES, SPIES AND STOCKHOLM SYNDROME

### FINBAR DWYER

NEW ISLAND

LIFE IN MEDIEVAL IRELAND:
WITCHES, SPIES AND STOCKHOLM SYNDROME
Published 2019 and reprinted 2022
by New Island Books DAC
16 Priory Office Park
Stillorgan
Co. Dublin, A94 RH10
Ireland

www.newisland.ie

First published 2013 as
*Witches, Spies and Stockholm Syndrome: Life in Medieval Ireland.*

Copyright © Finbar Dwyer, 2013

The author has asserted his moral rights.

PRINT ISBN: 978-1-84840-740-4
EBOOK ISBN: 978-1-84840-285-0

British Library Cataloguing Data. A CIP catalogue record for this book is available from the British Library.

Typeset by JVR Creative India
Cover design by New Island.
Internal illustration from Istockphoto.
Printed by Scandbook, Sweden.

New Island is a member of Publishing Ireland.

10 9 8 7 6 5 4 3 2

# Contents

# Acknowledgements

When Fred Cairns proofread a chapter of this book, his brief but succinct comments captured my relationship with grammar: 'The comma is not endangered. I have added many. Direct sentences are permitted. The word "however" flourishes dangerously and might be pruned.' There are many, including Fred, whom I have to thank for reintroducing the endangered comma and trimming back the voracious 'however'. My thanks go to Finbar Cafferkey, Sian Crowley, Katharine Gibney, Alison Gibney (and baby Cian), Cian O'Callaghan, Stephanie Lord, Ryan O'Sullivan, Paul Lynch, Peter McGuire, Paul Dillon, Paddy O'Byrne, Damon King, Tríona Sørensen, Lucy McKenna, Aidan Rowe, Daithí Mac An Mháistir, Bob Kavanagh, Dave Landy, David Robertshaw, Odhran Gavin and Cathie Clinton.

I would also particularly like to thank Matt Treacy, Oisin Gilmore and Eve Campbell, who read early drafts of the book, and Kevin Squires, for his editing, proofreading and map design. Cormac Scully and Eamonn Costello provided many of the pictures and ensured that they looked their best.

Writing a book proved far more difficult than I anticipated. Beginning life as an audio project, various incarnations of this book have been in the pipeline over the past few years, the completion of which would never have happened without Eoin Purcell and all the people at New Island.

The friendship, advice and support of a few people have been invaluable, in particular Stewart Reddin, Grainne Griffin, Carl Robinson and James McBarron. While there are many other people who helped me over the years, I would particularly like to thank Fergal Finnegan for the many hours of historical conversations and encouragement. I would also like to thank Alan Morkan, Dermot Sreenan, Aileen O'Carroll, Andrew Flood and Mark Malone, who have been a great source of advice, support and help along the way.

Fergal Scully deserves particular mention. He has been there through thick, thin and mountains of history books on the kitchen table, not to mention his invaluable proofreading of various articles as well as this book. Since I was a child I have been lucky enough to be surrounded by people who encouraged my interest in history: my uncles Colm and Sean and my late uncle Seamus, and also Mick and Peg Brennan. This book would never have happened without their passion and kind encouragement over many years.

Finally, I want to thank my family: my sisters Catherine and Ruth and brother-in-law Paul, who have encouraged me every step of the way, and my brother John, who has read and listened to countless hours of history audio and relentlessly pushed me to improve, and without whose advice and support I think it is fair to say this project would never have developed as it did. Most importantly I would like to thank my mother Máire, who has given me great support on all levels and who has been a source of inspiration throughout my life.

In memory of my father
Gerry Dwyer (1943-2013)

# Introduction

## I

$\mathcal{S}$hould someone from medieval Ireland walk into a bookshop in the twenty-first century (we won't even try introducing this fictional character to e-books) they would feel very neglected. The history sections of Irish bookshops are dominated by works on recent history such as the revolutionary period of 1913–1922 or the Troubles. The world of our medieval visitor scarcely gets a mention. As disappointing as this may be, our guest would surely feel worse off if they attempted to discuss medieval history in public. The history of the Middle Ages is so neglected that the only figure of renown is Strongbow, the man who led the Norman Invasion of Ireland in the twelfth century.

The scope of the few non-academic books available on medieval Irish history is generally quite limited. Most focus on the activities of half a dozen powerful families, which is by no means an accurate reflection of medieval society. There is little written about the lives of majority of men, who held no title or land, and even less about women. This book attempts to focus on ordinary people from the period by examining daily life. Indeed, so neglected are these people in history that many of the stories and people recounted in the following chapters haven't been heard of in centuries.

I have chosen to break from a traditional narrative in a chronological format as I feel it would have limited the scope of the book. While the second part of this introduction outlines a brief history of Anglo-Norman Ireland, I have structured the book itself around twenty-two independent chapters, each focusing on some aspect or person from medieval Ireland. While some are related, others have little in common save that they explore some aspect of medieval daily life.

There are also chapters that address universal themes, which crop up again and again throughout the book. Violence, famine and the Black Death were so all consuming and life changing (or ending) that it would be remiss not to refer to them constantly. It would be akin to writing a history of twentieth-century Europe and trying to avoid repeatedly mentioning World War Two.

The book is dominated by stories from the Anglo-Norman Colony in Ireland in the late thirteenth and early fourteenth centuries. This is inevitable for several reasons. Any medieval historian is naturally directed to this time period because it is covered by the greatest amount of in-depth contemporary sources. Coincidentally, it also happens to be arguably the most important period of medieval Irish history. The Norman colony in Ireland reached its geographical zenith in around 1270 and its economic height in around 1290. By the early fourteenth century, however, it was gripped by a crisis that would last at the very shortest estimate for several decades, but in some readings continued through to the 1660s or later.

The focus almost exclusively on life in the Anglo-Norman colony in Ireland to the neglect of the native

Gaelic society is largely down to sources. It would be impossible to reconstruct a picture of daily life in Gaelic Ireland accurately to the level of detail contained in the following chapters. With extensive parts of the west, north-west, midlands and Wicklow Mountains outside the power of the Anglo-Normans' governmental authorities, there are no documents such as court rolls or extensive property deeds from which we could accurately reconstruct daily life. Extending comparisons from colonial territory is dangerous given that the limited information we do have from Gaelic Ireland indicates that there were quite substantial differences between the two societies. Nonetheless, there are many Gaelic Irish people who feature in the following pages, often when they ended up on the wrong side of the law in Anglo-Norman colony.

## Terminology and Spelling

To avoid confusion, I have made some minor amendments to some quotations referenced in the text. There are quotes from thirteenth- and fourteenth-century sources, which at times can be confusing due to mistakes in the original text or the use of antiquated spelling. Where I felt that this only served to confuse, and the incorrect spelling had no specific meaning, I altered the word. The best example of this is the changing of 'divers' to 'diverse'.

In the thirteenth and fourteenth centuries, spelling was not as precise or uniform as it is today. Names were often spelt in numerous ways within the same account. Where this occurred, I chose one variant and used that throughout. The same applied as names changed through the century. This problem is at its most extreme when Anglo-Norman writers attempted to spell Gaelic Irish names. This has unavoidably led on a few occasions to very difficult names to pronounce, such as 'Octouthy', appearing in the text.

While the words 'English' and 'Irish' at times appear in direct quotations, I have tried to avoid using these terms where possible. Instead I have opted for 'Anglo-Norman' to refer to the colonists and 'Gaelic Irish' to the native population. The terms 'English' and 'Irish' have strong associations with modern nationalist political identities that are not useful when trying to understand medieval Irish history, when such associations did not exist.

# II

## Anglo-Norman Ireland

The following stories, drawn from daily life in the crisis-ridden Anglo-Norman colony of late-thirteenth- and fourteenth-century Ireland, at times lend credence to L. P. Hartley's aphorism 'the past is a foreign shore, they do things differently there'. Before we visit what can at times seem like a distant shore, it is important to explain the society in which these events took place: the society of our distant ancestors.

It was a society borne of a brutal invasion of Ireland in the decades after 1169. Many of the people whose lives are recalled in this book lived in a society that developed as a result of that invasion. Some, but by no means all, of the inhabitants of late medieval Ireland had their roots far from the shores of what became the Anglo-Norman colony on the island. Their ancestors had lived in Wales, England and northern France. Indeed, their multicultural origins were preserved in the French and English spoken alongside Gaelic Irish in the colonial towns. The time period this book focuses on, the late thirteenth century and early fourteenth century, was one of great crisis for these people and their colony. As we shall see, violence, war and famine were all too frequent. However, it was not always so; in their early days in Ireland, the Anglo-Normans seemed insurmountable.

Anglo-Norman Ireland began in 1167 when a small handful of mercenaries crossed the Irish Sea from Wales and landed on the south-east coast of Ireland. They accompanied Diarmait McMurrough, a deposed Gaelic Irish king of Leinster, who had hired them. Their mission was to restore him to power as king, but it would end with the conquest of most of Ireland. While they had come from Wales, many of the ancestors of these mercenaries had originated in Normandy in northern France, hence the term Norman. In 1066 these Normans had crossed the English Channel and conquered England, which gave rise to the term Anglo-Norman. In the following decades they had pushed west into southern Wales.

By the 1160s, when Diarmait McMurrough arrived looking for adventurers and mercenaries, the descendents of many of those who had settled in south Wales had fallen from political favour. In this environment they relished the chance to come to fight in Ireland, which offered fresh opportunities. The incentives were alluring; the leader of these mercenaries, the Earl of Pembroke, Richard de Clare, was promised lands and the hand of McMurrough's daughter Aoife in return for restoring the king to power.

Known to history as Strongbow, Richard de Clare was not among the advance party who landed in 1167. These first invaders initially posed little threat to the Gaelic order in Ireland. Few in number and lacking heavy cavalry, they failed to make a major impact, and Diarmait McMurrough had to sue for peace with his Gaelic rivals. These initial Normans, however, were merely the first wave. In 1169 they were followed by a major force of several hundred mercenaries, and McMurrough's cause appeared a more credible prospect. Finally, in 1170 Strongbow himself arrived at the head of a force of 200 knights and over 1,000 foot soldiers and archers. Ostensibly coming to fight as mercenaries, these men, many of whom were politically isolated in Norman Wales, started a process that irrevocably changed Irish history. The island would never be the same again.

Within a year they had reinstated Diarmait McMurrough, and Strongbow had married his daughter Aoife. Diarmait did not live long, dying in May 1171, leaving Strongbow, the most dominant figure in Leinster, at the head of a powerful army. Possessing Dublin, Waterford and Wexford, he was an increasingly powerful figure across Gaelic Ireland. Unsurprisingly, this threat drew down the wrath of Gaelic kings across the country.

In the summer of 1171 Strongbow was attacked by a large Gaelic alliance, but he successfully endured a siege in Dublin that lasted for several months. The fears of the Gaelic kings were well founded; later that year any pretext that these men were merely mercenaries evaporated as an out-and-out conquest began. This development was largely due to the arrival of the first English king on Irish soil in October of that year. Henry II, whose domains stretched from Wales through England to northern France, was increasingly dubious about the intentions of Strongbow and his followers in Ireland.

Wary of facing the prospect of a rival Norman kingdom on his doorstep, the king gathered an army and travelled across the Irish Sea. Henry II stayed in Ireland over the following winter, proclaiming himself overlord of Ireland and officially conferring Leinster onto Strongbow, thereby reaffirming their king–vassal relationship. He also went on to confiscate the kingdom of Meath, once home to the powerful southern O'Neill kingdom, and granted it to Hugh de Lacy. Whatever tenuous rights Strongbow had to Leinster through his marriage to Diarmait McMurrough's daughter Aoife, the confiscation of Meath was an outright act of aggression and conquest. It was to be the first of many – in the following six decades the Normans took advantage of internal divisions within Gaelic Ireland and conquered around 75% of the island. Their advance was aided by the disunity between the Gaelic kings in Ireland.

Prior to the invasion, Ireland was composed of around half a dozen independent kingdoms. Having long contested power between each other, they failed to find common cause against the Normans. This left a situation where individual Gaelic kingdoms fought the invaders often with little support from each other; while they enjoyed some victories, this strategy was disastrous. Having the advantage of heavy cavalry and superior military technology, some of the Norman victories were stunning. John de Courcy led 200 knights and conquered most of eastern Ulster in 1177 while the rest of Gaelic Ireland stood by and watched. Sixty years later Richard de Burgh destroyed serious opposition in Connacht with a fast-moving campaign in the summer of 1235. This culminated in a siege that saw the Normans force capitulation from a fortress on Loch Ce using catapults on floating platforms.

This invasion was not simply a military conquest; the lands that were conquered were completely transformed. This transformation was so extensive that the people whose lives are recalled in the following chapters would have struggled to recognise Ireland prior to the 1170s. In the decades after the invasion their ancestors had transformed the Irish landscape in almost every way imaginable as they carved out the Anglo-Norman colony in Ireland. The Gaelic society that had developed over the previous centuries was almost completely obliterated in the colonial regions. The Gaelic Irish elite were driven off the land or killed. Many withdrew into the mountains and bogs, poor lands in which the Normans had little interest. There they were left to eke out an existence.

★★★

While this appeared to be an easy solution in the twelfth century, it went on to create untold problems for the

Normans. These Gaelic Irish mountain settlements became reservoirs of resentment and ultimately resistance against Anglo-Norman rule in Ireland; events that provide the backdrop for many of the stories to follow. In the lands that the dispossessed Gaelic families had once ruled, the new Norman overlords reshaped almost every aspect of life. They imported settlers of all classes from England and Wales, who carved a new society into the landscape. Castles, of which there were few prior to the invasion, were erected across the island. Towns sprung up on what had been greenfield sites, while new ports were built throughout the country on Ireland's extensive river system.

One of the biggest changes in daily life was the reorganisation of agriculture. In Gaelic Ireland attitudes to land ownership and farming practices were radically different to those of Norman society. In the decades after the invasion, Gaelic collective land ownership was abolished, and conquered territory was reorganised into manors. These manors, which were both political and agricultural units, became the basis of rural medieval life in Anglo-Norman Ireland. They were populated with herds of sheep and cattle and sown with a wide variety of crops, the surplus of which was exported to England and the continent.

Impressive as this destructive creativity was, it did not happen evenly across the island. While most of Leinster, Meath, large parts of Munster and eastern Ulster were radically transformed, the Norman settlement in Connacht was very different. After the conquest of the province in 1235, the Lords of Connacht, the de Burghs, operated more like Gaelic kings than settlers. After failing to attract enough colonists, they struggled to maintain control over the Gaelic Irish and resorted to taking tribute rather than imposing direct rule in much of the region.

★★★

While the Normans unquestionably controlled and dominated this emerging colonial society, many Gaelic Irish people remained behind to work the lands. Many lived in collective family groups in the status of *betaghs*. These were the Gaelic Irish equivalent of serfs who were bound to the land (it is noteworthy that many had lived in similar servitude prior to the invasion). They were joined by large numbers of settlers from England, Wales and the continent. It is impossible to ascertain how many ultimately crossed the Irish Sea, but from the presence of Anglo-Norman and Welsh names in records, it appears that they were substantial in number.

Living side by side, intermarriage between the Gaelic Irish and the colonists was inevitable. Such relationships appear to have occurred at all levels of society: Strongbow married Aoife McMurrough, and later Hugh de Lacy married Rose O'Connor. This pattern continued right through the history of Norman Ireland: in the fourteenth century one of the most powerful men of the era, William 'Liath' de Burgh, married Finola O'Brien.

As Anglo-Norman society in Ireland took hold, laws and customs that mirrored those in England replaced the lawlessness and chaos that had followed the invasion. In the absence of the king, the Crown was represented by an individual known as the *Justiciar*, a figure usually drawn from the nobility in Ireland. This individual enforced his authority in a similar fashion to the king in England. In a world with very limited government apparatus, he travelled around Ireland holding court sessions and dispensing justice. Having the right to declare war, he also organised military missions during periods of revolt or conquest. He was aided in these duties by a council and a deputy-Justiciar. While the machinery of government was limited, there were numerous other officials such as a chancellors and treasurers who were aided by sheriffs, sergeants, coroners and bailiffs in their duties.

While the Justiciar enforced law and order in the name of the king, there were others with similar powers, albeit on a limited scale. By the mid thirteenth century there were several regions known as 'liberties' across the colony. These were in effect the property of a given lord, over which it was his duty and right to hold court and implement the law. He appointed a *seneschal* who oversaw his lands, held court and carried out similar duties to those of the Justiciar. The Church also retained its own liberties. This created a complex patchwork of legal systems, which often competed against each other for the right to try, punish, and profit from court cases.

While the Justiciar was theoretically the most important individual, powerful aristocrats could in reality wield more influence. By the early fourteenth century, for example, the de Burghs ruled nearly half the colonial territory in Ireland. Composed primarily of the Lordship of Connacht and Earldom of Ulster, these lands made Richard de Burgh the most powerful man on the island, and among the most powerful in north-western Europe. Regardless of the position or title he held, there was little a Justiciar could do if Richard de Burgh opposed him. When he engaged in lawless behaviour, no one could effectively restrain him, a problem that contributed to the increasing crisis that engulfed the colony in the later half of the thirteenth century.

While rural liberties were largely subject to the rule of a given aristocrat, the numerous towns across the island were proto-democracies. These settlements were ruled by elected mayors; the electorate was, however, an extremely limited group of people dominated by rich merchants. In the medieval world all rights and privileges, including voting rights in towns, strictly correlated to a given individual's wealth and property. The concept of universal suffrage did not exist.

The rights and legal protections the various court systems offered did not extend to the entire population. Many peasants were in effect tied to the land, with access only to a local court held on their manor that was presided over by their lord. If they had problems with him, there was little they could do. Similarly, most Gaelic Irish living within the colony had few rights. While they could be hauled before a court to answer charges, most could not take a case to these same courts. Indeed, a case could be dismissed from the court purely on the basis that the plaintiff was Gaelic Irish[1].

While it is tempting to look at this discrimination through the lens of modern racism, it should be noted that the concept of race in the medieval world was more fluid than it is today. The Normans appear to have paid more attention to language, dress and identity than ancestry. Therefore it was possible for a Gaelic Irish person to cross the divide and be afforded the rights of an Anglo-Norman settler, something unimaginable for an African-American in some US states in the nineteenth and early twentieth centuries.

## Crisis hits the colony

During its first century, Anglo-Norman Ireland expanded and was regarded as a success from the point of view of the colonists. Conversely, from the perspective of the Gaelic Irish, the century between 1170 and 1270 was one of unmitigated disaster. By the middle of the thirteenth century, the only Gaelic kingdom that had not been dismembered was that of the powerful O'Neills in western Ulster. Though the colony reached its greatest territorial extent in the mid thirteenth century, within a few decades it would be wracked by war and internal divisions that had their roots deep within the colonial structure.

The feudal society that took hold in Ireland was initially dominated by a handful of extremely powerful landowners who ruled over huge expanses of territory. However, what began as extremely large holdings were divided into much smaller plots during the course of the thirteenth century through a bizarre series of events that saw these lands broken up by inheritance. The most extreme case saw the lands of the heirs of Strongbow, the Marshall Lords of Leinster, carved up repeatedly. In 1245 Anselm Marshall became the last of his five brothers to die. Each of the brothers had inherited their father's title as Lord of Leinster, yet they had all subsequently passed away without an heir. After Anselm's death his family lands, including the Lordship of Leinster, were, in accordance with the law, subdivided between his five sisters or their heirs. Some of these sisters were dead with no male heirs, so their portions were divided between their daughters. Within a decade Leinster had been divided into over a dozen claims. This introduced many new aristocratic families into Ireland, whose primary concerns lay in estates in England, where they invested most of their energies.

While this division was not one of the root causes of the later problems that undermined the colony, it did exacerbate tensions when they arose in that some of the estates were poorly defended and badly managed, their owners having little interest in Ireland. There were some, however, who appointed very capable administrations to run their Irish lands, most notably the Bigod Lords of Carlow.

## Warfare between the settlers and the Gaelic Irish

While warfare was common between the Gaelic Irish and the settlers during the conquest and in the west, the year 1270 proved decisive when violence broke out in what had been the peaceful region of the Wicklow Mountains. Underlying this violence was an increasingly unpredictable climate with increased rainfall. This damaged harvests, and famine became more frequent. These food shortages forced the Gaelic Irish into action; starvation ensured that passivity was no longer an option. Raids on colonial settlements proved inevitable.

This presented a deeply troubling vista for the Anglo-Norman authorities. Revolt in Wicklow not only threatened the colonial capital of Dublin, but also New Ross, the busiest port, and the crucial communication corridor that was the Upper Barrow valley. While the violence in Wicklow was brought under control in 1282 with the assassination of the two McMurrough brothers who led the revolt, this was a decisive conflict. The underlying tensions that had surfaced proved irresolvable, and by 1295 the region was again at war.

These problems were accentuated by deepening tensions between the Norman aristocrats themselves. Violent rivalry had long divided the Normans in Ireland. In the later half of the thirteenth century these divisions reached crisis levels. Since the earliest days of their conquest, the Normans had failed to form a common aim or project in Ireland. Each of the major families pursued their own interests, even if that was to the detriment of wider Norman society. This mutual distrust had been fostered by successive English kings, who encouraged rivalries to prevent any one individual aristocrat from growing too powerful in a region that was difficult to control from England.

Increasingly through the thirteenth century these aristocrats saw each other as rivals for land and power. In an environment with few restraints there was little to hold these men back from acting as they pleased. To make matters worse, the royal policy of all four kings who ruled England between 1216 and 1377 was marked by an indifference to the colony in Ireland.

As warfare with Gaelic Ireland increased, these tensions between the Normans themselves broke out into full-scale civil wars in 1264 and 1294–5. On both occasions the de Burghs and Fitzgeralds devastated large parts of the colony over tensions arising from competing interests in the north-west. The rivalry between these families also contributed to another civil war in 1327. Little in the way of meaningful action was ever taken to punish the individuals involved, although, as mentioned earlier, there was scarcely anyone powerful enough to punish the de Burghs in any event. This inaction proved highly corrosive and destructive to colonial society, serving to reassure the nobility that they could act as they pleased.

By the late thirteenth century, the consequences of this laissez-faire attitude began to manifest itself in general lawlessness among the aristocracy. This ever increasing problem dominated the early Parliaments held in Ireland. The first binding Parliament was held in Dublin in 1297, and over the following decades there were frequent meetings. Usually attended by unelected nobility, powerful merchants and clergy, several Parliaments

– notably those of 1297 and 1310 – specifically addressed these issues. Unsurprisingly, the nobles did little to adopt any meaningful measures to punish their own lawlessness and reckless behaviour. This was, of course, not unique to the Anglo-Normans.

In a similar fashion, the Gaelic Irish across Ireland were riven by internal disputes. In Wicklow, for example, the McMurroughs, the traditional kings of the province of Leinster, increasingly fought with the O'Byrnes and O'Tooles. These two families had seen their power and prestige rise as they attacked colonial settlements – something that perturbed the McMurroughs. This constant feuding within Anglo-Norman and Gaelic Irish regions served to create a chaotic environment where several interlinked conflicts could be taking place at one time.

The myriad of problems that Ireland faced in the later thirteenth century were compounded by the outbreak of war between England and Scotland in 1296. During this conflict, Edward I and his successor Edward II drained Ireland of men, money and material. This substantially undermined the colonial economy. Having reached its height in the early 1290s, it began to contract rapidly under the weight of these problems.

Life failed to improve in the early fourteenth century, and Ireland was enveloped by a full-blown crisis when the war between England and Scotland spilled over into Ireland. In May 1315 Edward Bruce, brother to Robert the Bruce, the reigning King of Scotland, invaded Ulster. The invasion, which lasted until 1318, destroyed large amounts of land and devastated colonial society. To make matters worse, it happened during the most severe famine in medieval history.

Unsurprisingly, Norman Ireland struggled to recover from this catastrophe. Indeed, it was clear that the high point of the colony had long passed by 1320. This was symbolised by the death of Richard de Burgh, the Earl of Ulster, in 1326. Along with his cousin William 'Liath' de Burgh, the Earl had created the most powerful family that medieval Ireland had ever seen. In a development that reflected the wider malaise Anglo-Norman Ireland faced, the next generation of the de Burgh family was far less successful or united. William 'Liath' de Burgh's son Walter was starved to death by Richard's son and successor as earl in Northburgh Castle in 1331. Two years later this young earl himself was assassinated in an act of revenge. In the following years, de Burgh power, once an important foundation of the Anglo-Norman colony, crumbled as various factions of the family went to war against each other.

Meanwhile in the east, the colonial capital of Dublin faced its own crisis as the Gaelic Irish in the Wicklow Mountains grew increasingly powerful, attacking not only the Vale of Dublin to the south of the city but also the Barrow Valley. By the 1330s the Anglo-Norman colony was in full-scale retreat. Any hope of recovery was dashed in 1348 when the Black Death arrived in Ireland. In the following twelve months this plague killed 30–50% of the population, disproportionately affecting those who lived in urban settlements, who were primarily colonists. In the following decades, while the colony did not collapse as many predicted it would, it failed to recover and was beset by frequent warfare.

This brief sketch outlines the major players and developments in Anglo-Norman society in Ireland between 1170 and the mid fourteenth century. Like most histories of the period, however, it reveals very little about what it was like to live during this time. It doesn't mention the vast majority of people who tilled the land – the peasantry or women. The following stories reveal aspects of what it was like to live in this society as it was engulfed by famine, war and plague. This world of late medieval Ireland lends itself to a view that it was an exclusively male-dominated, violent, brutish, never-ending nightmare waiting to be put out its misery by the birth of the modern world. In reality, it was far more complex. While the violent stereotype is not far wrong, there was much more to the medieval world than bloodshed and political intrigue.

As we shall see, people in the medieval world were similar to us in some respects. They had friendships, and these friends played football, got drunk (a lot), fell in love, and even had sex! Of course, some aspects of this world do seem like the foreign country L. P. Hartley mentioned. Our ancestors lived in a world where a separation of Church and government was impossible; the king after all derived his power ultimately from God. Few could read or write, and most, if not all, firmly believed in the power of the supernatural. Nevertheless, it was on this distant shore, through the struggles of the people mentioned in the following chapters, that the modern world was born.

★★★

## Chronology of Major Events in Anglo-Norman Ireland

**1169**: The first major force of Anglo-Normans arrives in Ireland. They have been hired as mercenaries by the Gaelic King Diarmait McMurrough to reinstate him as king of Leinster.

**1171**: After initial successes, Henry II, the Norman King of England, arrives in Ireland. He proclaims himself Overlord of Ireland. The initial intervention becomes an invasion and conquest of Gaelic Ireland. The Norman colony of Ireland is established in the conquered lands.

**1235**: The final campaign of conquest takes place when Richard de Burgh leads a successful invasion of the Gaelic kingdom of Connacht.

**1250–70**: The area of colonised land now covers some 75% of the island.

**1270**: Provoked by famine, the first major revolt among the Gaelic Irish breaks out in the Wicklow Mountains. It is only brought under control in the early 1280s.

**1294–5**: 'The time of disturbance'. The supporters of the de Burgh and Fitzgerald families fight a major civil war, destabilising the colony in Ireland. Another revolt breaks out among the Gaelic Irish in Wicklow, again caused by famine as well as wider political instability.

**1296**: War breaks out between England and Scotland – a war that saw the Anglo-Norman colony drained of resources. This, along with increased Gaelic revolt and internal tensions, pushes the colony towards crisis.

**1315**: The war in Scotland is carried over into Ireland when Edward Bruce, brother of the King of Scotland, Robert the Bruce, invades Ireland.

**1315–18**: Ireland is hit by the worst famine of the medieval period. Cases of cannibalism are reported.

**1318**: Edward Bruce is killed at the battle of Faughart in Louth. The Scots invasion ends, but the Anglo-Norman colony lies in ruins after three years of war and famine.

**1327**: A major civil war breaks out between rival Anglo-Norman aristocrats in Ireland. The de Burgh and le Poers fight the Fitzgeralds and Butlers; Kilkenny and Tipperary are devastated. The colony is shrinking on an almost yearly basis as the Gaelic Irish enjoy increased successes.

**1333**: William de Burgh is assassinated by his own liegemen in Ulster. He was the third Earl of Ulster and son of Richard de Burgh (who had been the most powerful Norman aristocrat in medieval Irish history and died in 1326). His death triggers a civil war between various factions of the de Burgh family. The decline of the most powerful Anglo-Norman family adds to the ever growing crisis in Ireland.

**1348**: The Black Death arrives in Ireland. In the following twelve months, 30–50% of the population are killed after contracting the disease.

**c.1370**: The colony is in a state of almost perpetual warfare; letters are regularly written to England prophesising a complete collapse of Anglo-Norman Ireland. While this fails to materialise, the colony is plagued by reoccurring warfare and fails to recover for centuries.

# 1

# The Lifeblood of Medieval Society: Violence

Pub culture has a long history in Ireland. In the Middle Ages taverns were popular, so much so that one of Dublin's streets was solely dedicated to such establishments: Winetavern Street. If contemporary accounts from England are anything to go by, however, the standard of the drink on offer wasn't up to much. The late fourteenth century English poet John Gower lamented that tavern-keepers watered down wines and resold poor quality drinks as upmarket wine.[2] Customers socialising in some of Ireland's more raucous medieval drinking emporia, however, had greater concerns than the quality of the wine. In 1302 a court in Wexford heard how a certain Felicia was trampled by a horse 'maliciously' driven through the tavern in which she was drinking[3], while in 1300 an unfortunate customer drinking in a tavern in Cork lost his left eye when a patron carelessly flung an oyster shell over his shoulder.[4] Unsurprisingly, given that alcohol was involved, more serious disputes broke out as well.

## Violence in Dublin Taverns

In the summer of 1310, as Dubliners enjoyed the long evenings, an argument arose between two patrons, Reymund Freysel and John Cachfrens, in one of the city's taverns. As in the case of many pub arguments, the tensions eventually dissipated when Cachfrens left the tavern to drink elsewhere. Unfortunately, he did not forget the incident but instead sat fuelling his anger with wine. When the sun set late on that summer's evening, he had reached boiling point and resolved to find Reymund Freysel. After rounding up a gang, Cachfrens intended to do far more than just discuss his differences with Reymund; he was going to put an end to the dispute once and for all by killing the man.

Medieval Dublin, however, was a small place. Scarcely forty-four acres were enclosed within the walled city and, unsurprisingly, word filtered back to Reymund that his life was now in danger. Before he could make good his escape, however, Cachfrens arrived with his accomplices, forcing Reymund to flee, taking a spear with which to defend himself. Seeing that his enemy was making an escape, Cachfrens and his gang followed in hot pursuit. In what now became a manhunt, Freysel did his best to escape through the narrow medieval streets. Moving rapidly on such surfaces, described by contemporaries as so 'destroyed and broken that passing through the city is irksome and costly to passengers'[5] was not easy. Unfortunately, Cachfrens and his followers caught up with their human prey. His senses no doubt dulled by alcohol, however, John Cachfrens ran directly at Freysel, not realising that he bore a spear. Before he could stop himself, he was impaled upon the point of the weapon. Inevitably, in a world where surgery was rudimentary and antibiotics were non-existent, he later died from his wounds.[6]

While this incident could be dismissed as a drunken argument gone too far, it was reflective of a deeper, more systematic (and to modern eyes, disturbing) attitude to violence in medieval society. Similar forms of aggression did not just happen when people were drunk in Dublin's back lanes. Many people saw violence as an acceptable way for human beings to relate to each other. Cachfrens' decision to murder Freysel, while fuelled by alcohol, was by no means unusual behaviour. While the court system tried to curb such activity, they enjoyed little success. Indeed, it occurred on all levels of society; even the political leaders of the era orchestrated horrific levels of violence on their rivals.

Widespread conflict had been part of life long before the Norman Conquest in 1160s. In the later thirteenth century, though, there had been increased resistance to the Norman occupation from the dispossessed Gaelic Irish, which resulted in an upsurge of violence, particularly in the east of the country.

## The Necromancer of Toledo

Indeed, systematic violence was so chronic in this period that some contemporaries viewed Ireland as one of the most violent regions in Europe. The fourteenth-century Bishop of Armagh, Richard Fitzralph, when addressing the Papal Court of Clement IV in 1349, used a colourful parable to explain the society in which he preached. Relating a story about Johannes de Toledo, a thirteenth-century cleric known as the Necromancer of Toledo, Fitzralph claimed that Ireland was the most violent place on Earth.

The Necromancer had reputedly asked the devil which country sent the most souls to hell. In response, Lucifer replied that it was Ireland because murder and theft were so widespread. In the bishop's own words, he explained that the 'two nations are always opposed to one another from a traditional hatred ... so much so that every day they rob and slay and kill one another: nor can any man make any truce or peace among them, for in spite of such a truce they rob and slay one another at the first opportunity.'[7] Fitzralph was by no means the first to acknowledge the ferocity of such violence in medieval Ireland. A century earlier, in 1242, his predecessor as Bishop of Armagh, a native of Cologne, Albert Suerbeer, referred to a church in his diocese as being built between two nations who had destroyed the region by their constant war. Suerbeer went on to refer to the 'insatiable hatred'[8] the Gaelic Irish and Anglo-Normans had for each other.

Tensions between the Gaelic Irish and the Normans were not the only source of mass violence. In fact, tensions between the Norman aristocrats who gathered large personal armies around them and fought each other over lands and power were at times worse. In 1327, serious fighting broke out between several noble families. In a conflict that was centred on Kilkenny and Tipperary, an estimated £100,000[9] of damage was inflicted on this region, equivalent to approximately twenty years of what would have been very respectable exchequer incomes for the entire colony in this period!

Such figures, however, hide the human cost of violence and the brutality people witnessed on a daily basis. In the 1320s, in one annal compiled by a Franciscan in Kilkenny, Friar John Clyn, hundreds of brutal deaths were recorded. In 1323, Edmund Butler, whose son would become the first Earl of Ormond, burned alive men, women and children who had sought refuge at the monastery of St Mullins[10]. The following year, his ally, Robert Cuanteton, massacred 200 Gaelic Irish at Thurles[11]. In 1325, the Gaelic

Irish O'Carrolls attacked and destroyed a number of Norman settlements in the Midlands, with an unknown number of casualties. 1326 saw a massacre of eighty people in Carlow. In 1327, the sheriff of Kilkenny, together with twenty others, was killed by the Brennan family in north Kilkenny. Finally, to close what was only a moderately violent decade in a horrific century, James Butler, who had recently been made Earl of Ormond, attacked the O'Nolans in the Barrow Valley and 'wasted their lands and very near all their neighbourhood by fire'[12] in 1329. This was his response to the kidnapping of two men, one of whom was his brother. These are just the events recorded in one area by one chronicler, but the story was similar all across Ireland.

With leadership like this encouraging, organising and participating in massacres and violence on such a scale, it is little wonder that society was intensely violent. Indeed, the incident that occurred in the tavern in Dublin in 1310 between John Cachfrens and Reymund Freysel was mild compared with some of the other events happening regularly across the island. The story of Eynon Madoc, for instance, reveals a disturbing level of gratuitous violence within the context of daily life.

## Eynon Madoc: Vengeance and Violence

Little is known about Eynon Madoc's life prior to 1305, save that he had been declared an outlaw and a felon for an unknown reason. As his name suggests, Eynon was of Welsh descent. His family, no doubt, contained some of the thousands of colonists who had moved to Ireland to settle on the lands the Normans had conquered from the Gaelic Irish in the years after the invasion of the 1160s. Being declared an outlaw created severe problems for Eynon.

Being on the run meant that he was effectively no longer protected by the law, and so murdering him would not have been a crime. If he could stay alive, though, there were ways in which he could have this conviction nullified. Increasingly in the later thirteenth century, pardons were being offered across Anglo-Norman Ireland in return for service in the king's armies fighting in Scotland: a policy that did little to curb violence in society.

Until such time as he could be pardoned, however, Eynon seems to have been forced to steal to survive. This led him to the property of one Walter le Poer, a man who was himself away fighting for the king in Scotland at the time. Unfortunately for Eynon, while he helped himself to food and drink, he was caught in the act by le Poer's Sergeant, Mathew O'Ryan. O'Ryan tried to apprehend the thief, and a fight of sorts broke out. In the ensuing struggle, Eynon did manage to escape, but not before he was severely injured.[13]

Eynon fled to the house of his brother John Madoc, where his severe injuries enraged his relatives. John resolved to take vengeance against the man who had so injured his brother. Organising several other colonists, many of whom were of Welsh descent with names such as Rys Madoc, Iewan Robyn and Gwen le Waleys, into a band, John Madoc stormed the le Poer farmstead looking for O'Ryan. The attackers broke the doors of the hall, the chamber and other houses, took goods and 'wholly devastated his land'[14], but they could not find O'Ryan.

Three days later, Eynon Madoc succumbed to his wounds and died. Anger and a desire for vengeance again surged in his brother, and now John Madoc led a gang to the settlement of Carrickmcgriffin, where they finally caught up with Mathew O'Ryan. In an act of unbelievable barbarity, they dragged O'Ryan from the house in which he sat out into the public street. There, in full public view, they beheaded him. In a final act of humiliation, they stripped the corpse naked, stealing any belongings in his possession. There is little evidence that this act was viewed as being particularly heinous, which is indicative of the level of violence tolerated in medieval society.

When John Madoc and the others appeared before a judge, they successfully evaded convictions. After dragging out the case, they finally argued that O'Ryan was a felon himself, which legitimised the action. Mathew O'Ryan's Gaelic Irish background would have unquestionably played a role in the case; discrimination against Gaelic Irish people was a common feature in the colonial legal system. On one occasion when a case was being heard, many of the accused didn't bother turning up to court because they were fighting with the Earl of Gloucester's army against the Gaelic Irish in the Slievebloom Mountains. The court record noted that their presence in the army was integral to the security of the colony. The fact that Anglo-Norman society was dependent on such men was indicative of the wider attitude to violence. Eventually, the case was deferred indefinitely.[15]

While it seems incredible to us that the brutal murderer of Mathew O'Ryan could be treated with what amounted to a laissez-faire attitude, the use of violence was increasingly one of the ways in which people resolved disputes. The act itself was rarely questioned; the only issue was whether it was legal and legitimate.

That the Madoc family themselves would resort to such violent measures following the murder of Eynon Madoc is very much reflective of the society in which they lived. After all, twenty-five years later the Earl of Ormond, James Butler, would do far worse, devastating huge tracts of territory after his brother's kidnapping. Ultimately, for many there was almost no reason not to act violently when it achieved the desired objective of the perpetrator, be it vengeance, the pursuit of power or merely the possessions of a victim. This attitude to violence was accentuated by the actions of the king, who frequently offered pardons in return for renewed loyalty and military service, which removed many of the inhibitions and fears people had. Indeed, by 1317 the situation regarding pardons appears to have become intolerable. The Earl of Kildare, Thomas Fitzjohn – a man whose family had been pardoned themselves for what had been at times outrageous behaviour – wrote to the king pleading that officials should be prevented from granting 'pardons for the death of an Englishman, but that such Felons be judged according to the law'[16]. Presumably it was in response to this that Edward II banned such pardons, citing that 'others had been encouraged to commit crime on account of the facility of obtaining such pardons'[17].

Unfortunately, as will become obvious over the following pages, the banning of Royal Pardons failed to have much of impact. Violence was endemic throughout society, from men such as John Cachfrens and John Madoc all the way up to men like the Earl of Ormond, James Butler. Violence was an accepted mechanism to resolve differences and disputes in society, which made it an integral part of everyday life in medieval Ireland in a manner that we cannot comprehend today. Combining this with the cut-throat world of medieval politics proved to be an incendiary combination.

# 2

# The Revolt of Maurice de Caunteton and the World of Political Blood Sports

One the most famous political thinkers of the sixteenth century was the Florentine Niccolò Machiavelli. His political ideas have given rise to the term 'Machiavellian': a word synonymous with deceit, intrigue and cunning, all traits that he felt were necessary in an efficient ruler. While he wrote as the medieval world was giving way to the Renaissance and the early modern period, his ideas were still disturbingly relevant to thirteenth- and fourteenth-century Ireland. Indeed, they were not only advantageous, but arguably necessary in Anglo-Norman politics. When mixed with the widespread violence across society, politics in the Middle Ages often looked more like a blood sport than what we recognise as current affairs today. We have elections, canvassing and media appearances; they often resorted to murder, wars and kidnapping. Failure could easily result in losing a lot more than one's pride: frequently lives were on the line. Brutal as it may have been, these certainly made current affairs far more interesting.

The political world of the Middle Ages was completely unrecognisable when compared to its modern counterpart. In some respects, it was far more honest. The key players of the era did not pretend to act in the common interest. Instead, they were brutally honest about their aims and goals: to progress the interests of their family and their allies. Armed with such goals, major political disputes in Anglo-Norman Ireland took place not between political parties or ideologies but between rival families and their supporters over land, wealth and power. Family feuds and politics were inseparable, while the pride and power of one's family was the measure of political success.

As medieval Ireland entered its twilight years in the late thirteenth and fourteenth centuries, the great internal political tension of the period was between the de Burgh and the Fitzgerald families. The long-running dispute at times had the appearance of a Hollywood action blockbuster. What was essentially a conflict over land and power between the two families exploded on several occasions between 1264 and 1333. In one notable incident on 9 December 1294, the Fitzgerald patriarch John Fitzthomas kidnapped his opposing number Richard de Burgh, the Earl of Ulster and Lord of Connacht. Imprisoning de Burgh in his fortress of Lea Castle on the headwater of the River Barrow, Fitzthomas attempted to undermine de Burgh's power in his Lordship of Connacht. He eventually failed in what was a daring, if dangerous, gamble, but not before farms were burned, towns were looted and an unknown number of people were killed.

Strange as it may sound, this was what major political differences looked like in medieval Ireland — and it wasn't just the earls and lords who pursued their family's ambitions in such a ruthless fashion. Even at local levels, petty power struggles over relatively small amounts of land or wealth resulted in similar conflicts. Some of these were deeply personal, but violent political episodes escalated far beyond family feuds. This was often to the detriment of wider society, as was the case in a feud between the de Cauntetons and Talouns in the early fourteenth century.

It was into this world of violent rivalries that Maurice de Caunteton was born in the 1260s or 1270s[18], into a middle-ranking noble family with estates in Wexford, Cork and Limerick[19]. As was relatively frequent in the late thirteenth century, the Lord of Wexford, William de Valance, was an absentee lord. He chose to live on more valuable holdings in England. In their absence such lords appointed an official called a 'seneschal' who could run their estates in their name. Such a position gave men from minor noble families like Maurice a chance to extend his and his family's power. In the 1290s Maurice secured the position of Seneschal of Wexford, which made him in effect the manager of de Valance's lands and interests in the region. However, these were turbulent times in which to hold such an office. After John Fitzthomas kidnapped Richard de Burgh, it fell to Maurice to guide the Lordship of Wexford through the chaos that followed.

In the dog-eat-dog world of medieval politics, Maurice showed a degree of skill and ruthlessness that would have impressed Machiavelli. During the chaos of the de Burgh–Fitzgerald conflict of 1295, Maurice feared a potential siege of Ferns Castle, which he held for de Valance. Needing supplies, Maurice raided surrounding farms with little concern for the local population, who were facing one of the worst famines of the later thirteenth century.

On 3 February 1295, de Caunteton ordered his bailiff Alex Talemny to forcibly requisition the necessary supplies. This saw Talemny arrive at the home of a man called Richard, the chaplain in Enniscorthy, where he stole seven crannocks of meslin[20] and rye and fourteen crannocks of oats to provision the castle of Ferns. For the chaplain this was disastrous; grain was in very short supply and these stocks could not easily be replaced. While the chaplain did survive the famine, it would be two years before he was able to sue Talemny and de Caunteton in court to get redress. Showing contempt for the legal process and Richard the chaplain, Maurice simply didn't bother to turn up.[21]

Tempered in such volatile times, Maurice quickly learned that power lay in violence, and the law was something that he could deal with after the fact, if at all. Maurice failed, however, to grasp the limitations of his own power. This led to some poor decisions that would prove extremely costly.

In the early years of the fourteenth century, the political climate in Ireland continued to provide de Caunteton with opportunities. One of the major problems faced by the colonial administration in the early fourteenth century was the increasing power of the Gaelic Irish in the mountains north of Maurice's home in Wexford. Through surprise raids and warfare, the McMurroughs, O'Byrnes and O'Tooles were making life for the colonialists in the mountains unbearable, threatening huge tracts of land as far north as Dublin and as far west as the River Barrow. While in some years peace agreements were arranged with various Gaelic families, violence was as common a response. It was little surprise when, in 1302, several members of the de Cauntetons joined a force led by the deputy Justiciar Maurice de Rupefort to fight the Gaelic Irish in the Barrow valley.

This campaign took them to the lands of Richard Taloun following rumours that the rebel Gaelic Irish O'Nolans were holding cattle there. Richard himself was absent, but de Rupefort seized Adam Taloun and then appears to have allowed the de Cauntetons to take the possessions and animals of the Taloun family as spoils. The de Cauntetons thoroughly ransacked the farm, stealing away with a huge amount of Richard Taloun's property. This included animals such as oxen, cows, hoggets, goats and pigs. They also seem to have taken anything else they could move, including grain, cloth, household goods and weapons.[22]

When Richard Taloun himself returned home to find that the de Cauntetons had stripped his property bare, he was understandably outraged. Finding the guilty party can't have been difficult. Aside from the fact that they had been in the presence of the deputy Justiciar, the de Cauntetons can hardly have been inconspicuous as they travelled across the countryside with herds of animals and carts packed with loot.

Determined to get justice, Richard Taloun took a case against the de Cauntetons to the Justiciar's court later in 1302. He was successful in winning orders against several members of the family, including Maurice himself, who was to pay £100 in compensation and a further £20 in damages[23]. While Richard Taloun may have been pleased that the Justiciar (the highest official and king's representative in Ireland) had found in his favour, the case was by no means over. Maurice de Caunteton had already shown contempt for the legal processes of the colony and he would not easily relent. Soon Taloun faced stubborn refusal from a de Caunteton family who proved themselves a formidable and implacable enemy. Having seen the Fitzgeralds and de Burghs launch full-scale wars to protect their interests, the de Cauntetons were not about to relinquish their gains, no matter how ill-gotten: Maurice and his family simply ignored the court.

Had Richard Taloun seen sense he would have dropped the issue, but he was equally persistent. Although it took several years, he did successfully drag the de Cauntetons back before the courts in 1308, still seeking restitution.[24] On this occasion, Maurice was thrown in prison and crops were forcibly taken for sale to reimburse Taloun. This further inflamed the dispute, and Maurice fell back on the world experience he had gained through the 1290s. He had seen how violence had benefitted the higher nobility, and was more than willing to stand up to a royal administration that appeared increasingly weak. Maurice clearly felt that he had little reason to fear the courts as he soon began to undermine the legal process.

When the de Cauntetons' crops were seized, the sheriff claimed that he could find no one to buy the goods[25], indicating that potential buyers had been intimidated. To make their point more forcefully, Richard Taloun was viciously assaulted, in which his attackers 'waylay, beat, wound and ill treat him, and inflicted on him other outrages, to his heavy damage and against the peace'[26]. This was carried out by several members of the O'Ryan family and other Gaelic Irish who were acting on Maurice's orders.[27]

It was becoming increasingly obvious that Richard Taloun was not going to be reimbursed for the goods stolen, no matter what he did. Seven years had passed since the incident, and the de Cauntetons had fought the issue every step of the way. Taloun, however, had far too much faith in the legal system – or at least had too much faith in Maurice de Caunteton's willingness to abide by it. In 1309, Taloun again raised the matter before the deputy Justiciar William 'Liath' de Burgh. He was now seeking to pursue the case against legal officials involved. The entire affair was growing tiresome for Maurice de Caunteton.

He knew of easier and far more effective ways to end the dispute than intimidating buyers and Taloun himself.

On 17 June 1309, he sought out Richard Taloun and ended the seven-year-old feud by murdering him. This was no longer just a family dispute; Maurice was clearly defying the political authorities as well. While powerful men like John Fitzthomas could get away with similar behaviour, Maurice de Caunteton was not afforded such a privilege.

In killing Taloun he had committed a grave error, and soon afterwards the royal officials responded by having him declared an outlaw. This now put Maurice himself beyond the legal protection of Anglo-Norman Irish society. He was effectively shunned; anyone who aided him in any way was breaking the law. This was rigorously applied: after he had killed Taloun, Maurice had fled to his brother David de Caunteton, and he too was declared an outlaw. The situation cannot have been any easier for other members of the family; Maurice had at least two sons including a child who was only six years old when his father fled.[28] The pursuit of the boy's father was relentless, so any contact was extremely dangerous. When Maurice and his companions took refuge in a village on the lands of the priory of Glascarraig, which his ancestors had founded, the villagers were later fined the large sum of 100 shillings.[29] Life as an outlaw was difficult, but Maurice was about to make it a lot worse.

It was clear that, if they were to have any hope of surviving, Maurice and the de Cauntetons needed new allies. Having been rejected by Norman society, the de Cauntetons turned to the other major force in medieval Ireland and found allies among their one-time enemies: the Gaelic Irish O'Byrnes in the Wicklow Mountains, to the north of his lands in Wexford. With this new alliance, Maurice and his family 'openly put themselves at war with the King with standards displayed'[30]. His goal was far from clear, but it is likely that he hoped that if he caused enough trouble, he could secure a royal pardon. As crazy as this may seem, there was some logic to such an aim. The royal authorities in Ireland were increasingly short of funds, and financing major manhunts and military campaigns was an expensive business. Meanwhile, the king himself was generally willing to offer pardons in return for military service and renewed loyalty. In this environment, sometimes pardoning an individual like Maurice de Caunteton was the easier option.

Allied with the O'Byrnes, the de Caunteton gang effectively launched a revolt, committing what was later described as 'many murders, robberies and other evils'[31]. Unsurprisingly, his former Norman associates were less than impressed. In the early fourteenth century they were struggling to control the Gaelic Irish in the mountains, and the de Cauntetons were now busy doing their best to stoke up the flames of rebellion. Maurice himself should have known only too well what the reaction would be. Only a year previously he had joined a major campaign led by William 'Liath' de Burgh and Piers Gaveston in the mountains against the very same O'Byrnes with whom he was now allied. Predictably enough, by late 1309 a major military expedition was organised against the de Cauntetons.

The Justiciar was aided by Richard Taloun's family seeking vengeance. He also enlisted the help of the powerful Gaelic family the McMurroughs, who were themselves afraid of the rising power of the O'Byrnes. No expense was spared, with a total of £440[32] being spent, which amounted to 12% of the entire income for the exchequer in 1309.[33] Justiciar John de Wogan led the mission, no doubt reflecting a collective desire among many Normans to rid themselves of the threat. While Maurice had misjudged the situation in Ireland in terms of the wrath he brought down on himself, unbeknownst to everyone his strategy was working. While the Anglo-Norman authorities in Ireland geared up for a major military campaign, the king had written a pardon. He was unaware that Maurice was now in a race against time as to whether he could evade the Anglo-Norman authorities for long enough for the pardon to save him.

Maurice and his family were hunted down like animals, and were eventually cornered in the upper Barrow valley. Maurice had run out of luck and time. On Sunday, 5 October 1309, John de Wogan and Patrick de La Roche finally caught and killed him. David de Caunteton, his brother, did not fare any better: after being captured he was hanged in Dublin later that year. Unfortunately, the royal pardon en route from England failed to reach Ireland in time. In a world where politics was so lethal, many like the de Cauntetons miscalculated the risks, but others were more successful. A few years later, in 1312, the de Verdun family led a full-scale revolt in Louth, even defeating a royal army sent against them[34]. This worked out slightly better: although their lands were confiscated, they were returned after a few years of loyal service. The greatest losers in these events were often not the main protagonists or their families. While Maurice's sons lost their father, they were eventually allowed to inherit the family lands.

The tenants who lived on Maurice's estates were not so lucky. After he was killed the lands were undefended, and ultimately the tenants lost both their lands and homes. For many years this region of Wexford had been raided by the Gaelic Irish McMurroughs in the mountains to their north. While the McMurroughs had helped the royal authorities capture and kill Maurice, once he was dead they began to eye up the family estates.

By 1310, sections of the lands were described as 'ruinous and no one inhabits it or can inhabit it until much expense be incurred for its repair'[35]. The cause was the McMurroughs, who took advantage of the fact that Maurice had fallen foul of the Anglo-Norman authorities. These lands were deemed to be 'worth nothing because they lie uncultivated, nor does anyone dare to put hands to them on account of the Macmurghs [McMurroughs] who, after Maurice put himself at war against the King, preyed upon and devastated that land'[36]. The tenants were never able to return to these lands. Over twenty-five years later, in 1334, they were still described as being under the control of the Gaelic Irish.[37]

# 3

# Love and Marriage

## Stephen le Poer and Margaret Russell; a story of medieval 'romance'

I n the early fourteenth century, the aristocratic le Poer family had a notorious reputation for lawless behaviour. Among the most infamous members of the family was Andrew le Poer, a brigand who was executed in New Ross before 1305[38]. When several members of this family – led by the Baron of Dunhill, John le Poer, and a relation, the knight Stephen le Poer – arrived at the home of Reginald Russell in Mullinahone in County Tipperary in 1311, the latter fled, unsurprisingly, in terror. This gang were as dangerous as they were disreputable.

However, at Russell's farm in 1311 their criminal behaviour was not the usual brigandage for which the le Poers were increasingly renowned. If anything, it was a crime of passion. In a story akin to an epic romance, Stephen le Poer had arrived to elope with Margaret, the wife of Reginald Russell.

Stephen was in love with Margaret, or so he claimed. Margaret had apparently said of Stephen that it was he 'whom she loved above all'[39]. A later court heard a handmaid claim that Margaret had written to Stephen and agreed to marry him. Seemingly, Stephen was just acting on his passion for Margaret; a passion that she seemed more than willing to reciprocate. The story seems worthy of one of the great love epics of the age, but alas the tale of Stephen and Margaret was no Tristan and Isolde. Instead, it was a grubby story of violence and coercion, but one that was far more revealing about love and marriage in the medieval era than any epic.

A later court case in Waterford revealed the reality behind the events. Stephen had turned up with his notorious relatives and raided Russell's lands and carried Margaret away 'against her will'[40]. Far from being in love, Margaret was terrified. Seemingly in a hopeless situation, she received aid from an unlikely source when the Baron of Dunhill, John le Poer, came to her aid. He had only helped Stephen as he had been misled as to the details of the case.

The following day the Baron had to escort Margaret to Dungarvan Castle for safety, but Stephen and the other members of the gang pursued them. Six days passed before Reginald, Margaret's husband, eventually arrived at Dungarvan Castle to take his wife home. Disturbingly, he only did so after John le Poer, the Baron of Dunhill, had testified that Margaret had not been raped.[41]

This story reveals what was at times the reality of how women were treated behind the myth of medieval romance. Margaret was abducted, she had to be protected for six days against a marauding gang, and then after the traumatic ordeal was only 'saved' by her husband after the Baron of Dunhill had 'sworn that neither Stephen nor any other who had come there with them had caused dishonour to Margaret'[42]. This tale lays bare what was often the underpinning of medieval marriage and attitudes to women: they were largely viewed as property. Margaret was property both to Stephen, who felt he had the right to abduct her, and to her husband Reginald, who was concerned she had not been raped, an issue that would have tarnished his honour. No one in the situation, save the Baron of Dunhill, showed any concern for Margaret herself.

Unfortunately for women in medieval Ireland, such attitudes were not unusual. When wealthy women were married, the event was in essence a financial transaction, and one over which most women had very little control. Most weddings were preceded by the agreement of a dowry, a financial accord that saw the brides carry property and wealth into her future husband's family. In aristocratic families, marriage frequently saw women used as a political bargaining chip to forge alliances between powerful houses. Love or happiness was by no means a necessary prerequisite.

## Marriages of Inconvenience

One of the most famous marriages in late medieval Ireland was a case in point of a politically advantageous union. Through the late thirteenth century, Anglo-Norman Ireland was devastated by a civil war between the Fitzgerald and de Burgh families. This reached unprecedented levels during an event known as 'the time of disturbance' in 1294–1295, when the Fitzgeralds kidnapped Richard de Burgh.

In the aftermath, substantial pressure was placed on both families to end the feud, which was beginning to endanger the entire Norman colony in Ireland. Over the final years of the thirteenth century a deal was cobbled together between the respective leaders of both houses – Richard de Burgh, the Earl of Ulster, and John Fitzthomas, the Lord of Offaly. As part of this deal, two of de Burgh's daughters, Joan and Catherine, were married to two members of the Fitzgerald family, Thomas Fitzjohn and Maurice Fitzgerald. The fact that Joan de Burgh was still an infant when it was arranged was irrelevant (the marriage could not be enacted until 1312 when she had come of age).

These strategic marriages could leave daughters estranged from their families if the political environment changed. In 1302 another of Richard de Burgh's daughters, Elizabeth, married a family ally, Robert Bruce, a Scottish noble. Four years later, Robert seized the throne of Scotland for himself; by 1306 he was at war against the English King Edward II. By extension, he was also at war with Elizabeth's father, Richard de Burgh, who was among the most powerful nobles in Edward's kingdom. In 1315 King Robert instructed his brother Edward to carry this war into Ulster, Elizabeth's homeland, which he utterly devastated before routing Elizabeth's father at the battle of Connor in September 1315.

While only the elite could engage in such politically strategic and potentially calamitous marriages, financial aggrandisement was a motivating factor right through medieval society. In 1307, Margery Fleming married David le Crik for a more modest dowry of twenty marks, while David promised he would give Margery over 100 acres of land. While by no means meagre, this was far from the vast estates transferred when Elizabeth de Burgh married Robert Bruce in 1302. Incidentally, Margery's marriage contract ended up in the Justiciar's court when David slept with two of Margery's cousins and the Flemings tried to pull out of the deal.[43]

Essentially business contracts, marriages could be arranged in the bluntest fashion, leaving the woman involved with no illusions as to how her male relations viewed her. One such contract, which saw Lucy de Alneto marry William de Marisco, was devoid of any semblance of caring or affection. Alexander de Alneto, Lucy's father, agreed a deal with de Marisco that included a clause of what was to happen should the bride die without an heir. The contract read: 'Should the said daughter die without an heir, said William to have the manor [of Chamlea] for 6 marks yearly, until he receives the 47½ marks or grantor [Alexander] have paid his chattels'[44]. Creating a caveat for Lucy's death before she had given birth to an heir reveals as much about attitudes to women as it does about the high rate of mother and child mortality.

To ensure that marriage contracts were fulfilled, men dominated the lives of their female relatives. It was illegal for a woman to marry without the consent of her father – or, in the case of his death, her eldest brother. For wealthy women with no significant surviving male relative, her marriage was placed in the hands of the king, who decided when and whom she would marry. Some women ignored these laws. Margaret, whom we met earlier, married Reginald Russell without the permission of the king after her first husband had died. For this, Margaret's lands were taken by the king, and she was fined according to their (significant) value before they were returned to her.[45]

## Married Life

Married life could be very difficult for women. Because of biological necessity, wealthy women married young, sometimes as young as fifteen. Some women spent the following two decades of their lives pregnant, recovering from birth and having more children. When Margaret de Guines married the Earl of Ulster, Richard de Burgh, around 1281, she spent the following twenty years giving birth to the ten children who survived infancy. These were very possibly accompanied by several miscarriages as well as children who died at childbirth or in early infancy, a very common feature of medieval life. When she died in the early fourteenth century she had spent most of her life bearing children, an experience not uncommon for many wealthy medieval women. Whether women from poorer backgrounds in Ireland gave birth as frequently is almost impossible to tell due to a lack of records. These women had to factor in financial concerns, as each extra child was another mouth to feed.

It is little surprise that some of these relationships produced mismatched marriages that were unable to fulfil the emotional and sexual desires of the couple involved. The lyrics of a song surviving from the fourteenth century 'The Maid in the Moorland' voices such frustrations:

*Alas, how can I sing?*
*My pleasure is gone.*
*How can I live with that old man?*
*And still keep my lover,*
*Sweetest of all things?*[46]

These loveless relationships in the late medieval period did not mean that people were emotionless. They had the same desires as we do today. Often trapped in these relationships, some fulfilled their desires outside of marriage.

## Adultery

While adultery was severely frowned upon, from surviving evidence it appears it was not that unusual. For women, due to the patriarchal nature of society, such relationships could be difficult, and the implications could be serious. Evidence of extramarital affairs, which are by their nature clandestine, was rarely recorded. We do have some snippets, usually when people were caught or when things went wrong. This is how we have an insight into the relationship between a woman called Basilia and Stephen le Clerk.

In the early fourteenth century, Basilia married John Don, who, shortly after their marriage, travelled overseas, leaving Basilia at home. In his absence she struck up a relationship with Stephen le Clerk, and as the records state that 'they lay together at their will for the whole time that John was in the parts beyond sea'[47]. They failed to keep their relationship secret, and when John returned home he was told of the affair by his friends and neighbours. John warned Stephen to stay away from his wife, but no sooner was he away again than Basilia and Stephen resumed their relationship. On returning to hear the same story of the affair, John resolved to take decisive action. Pretending he was heading away again, he instead remained at the house of a friend, having requested a local tavern owner to inform him if his wife and her lover met up.

Sure enough, later that evening Stephen arrived in the tavern, followed shortly by Basilia. Word was sent to John, who arrived to the tavern at the head of an armed gang where the two lay together. Although Stephen tried to escape, John caught him and cut off his testicles, thereby ending the relationship in a rather direct manner.[48]

While most affairs didn't end in such a dramatic, painful or decisive fashion, this was not the only story of married women sleeping with men who weren't their husbands. While this is a far cry from the medieval notion of chivalry and courtly romance, it was nonetheless a relatively predictable reaction in a society that produced loveless marriages. These illicit relationships were often where people could actually meet partners of their choosing rather than people chosen for them due to social, political or financial reasons.

# 4

# Famine

O n 27 June 1331, Dublin witnessed one of the more unusual events in the city's long history. Towards evening, a large herd of several hundred whales beached themselves in Dublin bay close to mouth of the River Liffey. While a similar event would provoke fascination and concern for the whales today, in 1331 within the walls of Dublin there was little interest in the welfare of beached and soon to be doomed whales. Indeed, the people themselves were struggling to survive.

Over the previous twelve months Ireland had been hit with extreme weather. A contemporary noted that during 'May right up to [the following] February it was excessively wet, full of rain and wind so that summer and autumn seemed almost to have become the winter period'[49]. If this wasn't bad enough, late in 1330 the situation deteriorated further when two ferocious storms swept across the country. On 25 November, and again on 23 December, an eyewitness described a 'violent and dreadful wind'[50] that 'dispersed haycocks, destroyed houses and caused much damage'[51]. In Meath, bridges of both timber and stone were washed away as the River Boyne flooded[52], while the Franciscan friaries at Trim and Drogheda were severely

51

damaged[53]. A human cost was inevitable; chroniclers reported the deaths of the wife and daughter of Lord Milo de Verdun, who were killed when a wall collapsed on them. The occasional noble death here or there from collapsing buildings, however, was not of the greatest concern to the public in late 1330; they were well aware that worse was to come.

Poor weather in summer and autumn in the Middle Ages had dire consequences. The direct result was a poor harvest, which itself would lead to food shortages. In years such as 1330, when bad harvests were particularly severe, famine and death followed. Those cleaning up in the aftermath of the storms of late 1330 were conscious that what limited food supplies they had left would run out long before the next year's harvest would be gathered. This would translate into the deaths of thousands in the following twelve months.

The impact of such food shortages was terrifying for those who lived through them. They not only carried away thousands through starvation, but they also ripped medieval society apart. Famine was accompanied by huge social upheaval; it destroyed community solidarity, drawing out the worst in people as the starving survived by whatever means were necessary. Terry Jones and Alan Eriera's book, *Medieval Lives*, detailed the final stages of starvation in the following manner: 'The victim can see and feel their body withering away and becomes obsessed with food. Indifference and apathy replace compassion for their starving neighbours, friends and family. Mothers have been known to snatch food from the hands of their children. Cannibalism is not uncommon. Eventually when a person has lost about 40% of their body mass death is inevitable'[54].

In Dublin, and indeed across Ireland by June 1331, this haunting spectre of famine materialised as shortages pushed grain prices up, placing many essential foods such as bread beyond the reach of the poor. The population must have been mindful that many would soon engage actions such as those outlined above.

The memories of what had happened during previous famines were unforgettable. In 1295 the poor of the Dublin were reported to have eaten the bodies of executed criminals[55], while twenty years later cannibalism was again reported during the worst famine of the era, which lasted from 1315 to 1318.

## Increasing Famine in the Late Thirteenth Century

Indeed, the famine of 1330 was just the latest in a long line that had wreaked havoc in Ireland in the late thirteenth and early fourteenth centuries. The island had seen an increase in famine since the early 1270s. While there was a brief respite in the years leading up to the mid 1290s, several famines followed in quick succession – 1295, 1310, 1315 and 1330–31. Unquestionably the worst of these had been the famine of 1315, in which around 10% of the English population died.[56] In Ireland, the mortality rate during this period was probably substantially higher, given that starvation was accompanied by Edward Bruce's invasion, which saw a Scottish army devastate vast tracts of land, using scorched earth tactics in some of the most fertile areas of Ireland.

A city shaped by such experiences was perhaps the worst place possible for an unsuspecting herd of whales to beach themselves in 1331. While the extent of the starvation may not have been as bad as 1315, the population was desperate, and the reaction of Dubliners was predictable. Thinking about human survival rather than animal welfare the citizens, led by Justiciar Anthony de Lucy, went to the beach and butchered some 200 whales, the meat of which 'no man was forbidden to carry away'[57].

While the whales' tragedy was the city's saviour, averting disaster in 1331, this was an unusual experience. Normally when famines struck in the Medieval period, people starved; international aid as we know it was non-existent. People were often left to their own devices, and as an increasingly emaciated population faced death, desperation took hold and people contemplated actions they would normally regard as unthinkable. Theft became widespread.

The immediate cause of desperation during famines was the rising cost of food. When crops failed this did not mean there was no food, but rather that there was less food, which caused prices to rise. During the famine of 1310 the price of wheat reached sixteen shillings per crannock (the standard measurement of the day) before soaring to twenty shillings per crannock[58] in early 1311. This was a dramatic increase from the normal price of four shillings per crannock. These price increases were also reflected in other crops like oats and corn. Such price rises pushed the price of basic foods like bread through the roof. While many faced starvation, famines did not affect everyone equally. The rich could afford such increases in food prices. During the great famine of 1315–18 the wealthy monks of Durham and Norwich Cathedral priories did not need to alter their food intake as they could easily meet the shortfalls and increased prices.[59] The majority, of course, did not have this luxury; they had to battle with neighbours, friends and in some cases their own families for survival.

## Social Upheaval

Facing starvation, the theft of foodstuffs increased, as did raids on mills and farms where grain, an increasingly valuable commodity, was stored. Many who would not normally have resorted to stealing were forced to take such desperate measures.

In October 1310, Richard Bonde 'burglariously entered the mill of Geoffrey Coulmolyn by night and stole of the corn of John Geffrey'[60]. Richard went on to steal half a crannock of wheat and corn belonging to Robert Straff, and before the night was out he had broken into the kiln at the Abbey of St Thomas the Martyr at Newbury as well. Kilns were used to dry corn, making it an attractive target for starving people. Richard was caught, charged and found guilty, but, in what was an unusual display of compassion, he was pardoned. In the court's view he had been motivated by 'excessive poverty and hunger' because in the 'summer last past, there was great dearth in this land'[61]. They also noted that Richard had no previous convictions. He agreed to pay an unknown fine[62], indicating that he was a relatively wealthy man.

In March 1311, Richard Stakepoll was likewise charged and convicted of robbing four hams worth four shillings from the house of John Seys. The jury noted that his crime was the result of 'excessive want and poverty', and that he was not suspected of other misdeeds. He and his family were able to afford the substantial fine of twenty shillings[63], again indicating a degree of wealth. The very poor, as we shall see, faced far harsher sentences.

The poor, many of whom struggled in the best of times, and were most likely to steal during famines, were shown little sympathy. In the summer of 1310 John Baynguard was arrested in Kildare for using a ladder to scale the walls of the priory of Tamelynbeg and steal malt, corn and wheat from the kiln, mill and grange. John had been doing this for a year and half (there had been food shortages in 1308 as well)[64]. By what the court called his 'diverse turns',

John robbed forty shillings worth of food from the nuns over the eighteen months, indicating that he was possibly living off his thefts. Having been found guilty, he received no compassion, the court deciding simply to 'let him be hanged'[65].

On 25 February 1311, a miller from Waterford named David was charged that he wandered by night, breaking into pigeon houses. In two separate incidents, David stole pigeons worth a total of five shillings, twelve pence. He was convicted of the robberies, and several others, called a common robber, and was to receive no clemency even though he had been stealing food during a famine. He had no property or chattels, and received a death sentence. As with John Baynguard, David the miller too was hanged.[66]

Aside from medieval authorities punishing the victims of starvation, there were even darker aspects to famine as solidarity between people collapsed. While the wealthy were better positioned to survive increasing food prices, the violent were also better able to find food as they could prey on the weaker and more vulnerable in society. In June 1310, on the same day John Baynguard was sentenced to death, the Justiciar's court heard the details of one such case. With Ireland increasingly engulfed by food shortages, Hugh De Hereford was part of a gang that turned up to the house of Richard Spiryn in Clane, County Kildare on the night of 16 April. There they found Richard and his wife eating their last remaining food, some bread and fish. The gang demanded the food, but Spiryn refused, saying that 'he had no other food for himself and his wife'[67]. Spiryn then, in what appears to have been an effort to defuse tension, broke the bread and offered some to Hugh de Hereford. Hugh rejected the offer, instead demanding all the food and taunted Spiryn by feeding the bread he had offered to his dog. After this, the gang viciously beat and stabbed Spiryn before fleeing the scene. In the aftermath the gang were pursued by townspeople of Clane, and Hugh de Hereford was killed by an axe blow to the head.[68] Similar activity increased as food became ever scarcer and more valuable.

## Profiteering

Increasing prices also saw people attempt to profiteer from the food shortages. Among the best positioned to do this were bakers, and amidst the famine of 1310 the bakers of Dublin were found guilty of producing bread of 'false weight'[69]. This was a process by which they mixed flour with cheaper ingredients, increasing their profit margins. Such acts could produce violent reactions at the best of times, but with a starving population the bakers were lucky to escape with their lives. Instead of death sentences they received 'a new kind of torment which had never been seen there before'[70]. The bakers were tied to the tails of horses and drawn along the hurdles – wooden meshes that lined the city streets. While not a fatal punishment, the pain and humiliation no doubt ensured that the bakers would think twice before tampering with the flour quotient in bread again.

While many towns across medieval Ireland suffered the social upheaval of robberies, thefts, assaults and starvation during periods of famine, those living close to the Wicklow Mountains faced a potentially even greater problem. After the Norman Conquest in the twelfth century, the Gaelic Irish from Kildare, north Wexford and the regions surrounding the mountains had been disinherited, and many had been forced deep into the inhospitable uplands of Wicklow. Even at the best of times life in the mountains was hard; during periods of famine it was intolerable.

Desperation forced them to launch large-scale raids against Norman settlements close to the frontiers. During the famines of 1270, 1295, 1310 and 1315, the starving Gaelic Irish raided Norman settlements in incidents that often sparked wider conflicts. While for the Gaelic Irish these raids were a matter of survival, those living in colonial settlements saw their homes and farms destroyed. It would often take months, and in some cases years, for peace to be restored.

While such raids were generally limited to the frontiers, very few could totally escape the effects of famine, whether direct or indirect. Death and starvation were the ultimate fates of a minority, but even those who survived would have been touched to some degree by robberies, thefts, violence and in some cases even outright warfare. Famine cast a large and fearful shadow over life in medieval Ireland, particularly after 1270 as the climate became increasingly wet. While people dreaded its arrival, famine can only have been greeted with a degree of fatalism that we would find difficult to comprehend today. In the absence of international relief efforts, and aside from unique events like the beaching of whales in Dublin in 1331, the poor generally starved. Survivors bore the effects of starvation on their health for the rest of their lives.

# 5

# Reverence, Riots and Religion: The Church in Medieval Ireland

The town of Leighlinbridge in County Carlow, known in the fourteenth century as New Leighlin, was an important medieval crossing point over the River Barrow. In the early fourteenth century, among the more notable travellers who passed through the town was His Excellency William Fitzjohn, the Bishop of Ossory. In March 1305, Fitzjohn graced the inhabitants of New Leighlin with his presence, in what proved to be a memorable visit.

Fitzjohn was travelling from his diocese of Ossory, on the western side of the Barrow, to the town of Castledermot, further upstream in County Kildare. Given the increasingly dangerous times, the bishop travelled in convoy with an armed entourage. As the convoy made its way through Leighlinbridge, it was increasingly spread out. One of the Bishop's valets, Simon Purcell, and his serving man straggled behind. As the pair reached the house of Robert le Tannere, Purcell's serving man was attacked by a dog that had darted from the house. Purcell reacted quickly and struck the dog with a spear.

Watching the scene unfold from his house, the dog's owner, Robert le Tannere, reacted furiously. Rushing out, he attacked the serving man with a piece of wood, seriously injuring him in the face. The situation quickly escalated, and Le Tannere, outnumbered, retreated and took refuge in his home. Meanwhile, Purcell was joined by another man from the archbishop's convoy, and together they attempted to break down the door of the house. Fearing for his life, le Tannere and his wife fled their home and sought the aid of neighbours.

The townspeople quickly rallied and surrounded the men at le Tannere's door, attacking them with sticks and stones. A full-scale riot quickly ensued, and on hearing the commotion the Bishop William Fitzjohn doubled back. Arriving on the scene, the bishop, appalled by the violence, tried to gain influence over the situation using his religious authority. Invoking a benediction, a plea for divine help, Fitzjohn told the riotous crowd to 'cease doing evil to his men'[71].

Divine powers or not, the bishop was ignored, and if anything the riot intensified. When the hostilities finally ended, one of his valets, Michael de la Lyserne, was so badly beaten he was feared to have suffered fatal wounds. Another man had been struck by an arrow, while the bishop himself was wounded with a stone in the melee. Within a few days the issue ended up in court, and unsurprisingly the townsfolk were heavily punished. Not only were they collectively fined 100 marks, but several were committed to gaol.[72]

While the story reveals Robert le Tannere's love for his dog and his hot temper, more interestingly it discloses a lot about medieval attitudes toward religious figures. Townspeople rioting against a bishop over an issue like a dead dog is not exactly what we would expect in medieval Ireland. Such incidents challenge popular notions of the piety of medieval Christians, who reputedly fought wars for their beliefs at the drop of a hat.

The riot in Leighlinbridge illuminates the complex relationship between medieval people, the medieval Church and the Christian ideals that formed those beliefs. While undoubtedly the majority in medieval Ireland held their Christianity very dear, they were not always enamoured with the Church hierarchy. Given the reputation of the bishop of Ossory, this is not as surprising as it might first appear.

## Church Leaders

William Fitzjohn was by no means an inspirational or venerable Church leader. His personal life did not correspond with the religious beliefs he claimed to espouse, and in 1322 the bishop faced accusations of corruption. One particular rumour circulating at that time also claimed that he was 'the father of fourteen spurious daughters, to whom he has given dowers and married them to rich and noble men, thereby increasing his power and oppressing the clergy and people of his province'[73]. There may in fact be some truth to these claims. In 1317, following his replacement as Bishop of Ossory, his successor Richard Ledrede condemned the practice of priests having concubines in the diocese. While FitzJohn was far from a paragon of virtue, his faults were by no means unique among medieval Church leaders.

One of the most prominent religious figures of late thirteenth-century Ireland was the Archbishop of Dublin, Fulk de Sandford. He reigned as bishop for fifteen years between 1256 and 1271, when he died. Over a decade later another family member, John de Sandford, rose to the same position. The fact that de Sandford was Fulk's illegitimate son certainly raised a few eyebrows.

Senior clergy also fell to other worldly temptations. In 1325 Alexander de Bicknor, the Archbishop of Dublin and one-time treasurer of Ireland, was convicted of forging royal accounts. As a consequence, his lands and possessions were confiscated[74]. Given this context, it is perhaps more understandable that William Fitzjohn's pleas for peace at Leighlinbridge not only fell on deaf ears, but served to fuel the blazing anger of the irate townspeople. The source of resentment against the senior clergy was not limited to illicit liaisons, hypocrisy, double standards and moral failings. Bishops and archbishops were immensely wealthy figures, ruling over the vast estates that accompanied their position.

The Archbishop of Dublin was illustrative of the vast wealth and power of the clergy in medieval Ireland. While presiding over the spiritual needs of his diocese, he held approximately 50,000 acres of land in the city and county: almost 25% of the land in Dublin. In addition, he controlled significant estates in Wicklow.[75] Meanwhile, the other major religious institutions in Dublin owned an additional 50,000 acres. Thus, religious figures controlled almost half of the land mass of the county of Dublin.[76] Given the extent of their land ownership, the archbishops and priors acted as feudal lords to many poor peasants who struggled to eke out an existence. The Church's vast wealth was, in part, accrued from the work of these peasants, who tilled their fields and paid their rents. Inevitably, given their role as feudal lord, the religious elite frequently came into conflict with many of the faithful.

In 1313 Thomas Olongthy, the archdeacon of Cashel, appeared before the court of Walter de Thornbury to plead the case of Mathew Bryan, a prisoner accused of murder. While today we might expect a religious figure in such a position to plead for clemency, Olongthy's motivations were of an altogether different variety. The archdeacon was in fact demanding that the court turn the prisoner over to Church, which was keen to punish Bryan, which claimed that the crime was committed in its jurisdiction. The bishop's demand was acceded to, and the accused was turned over to the custody of the Church, whereupon he was taken to archbishop's prison. It was common in medieval Ireland for bishops and priors to maintain prisons and gallows upon which those convicted of capital crime would be dispatched. Consequently, the religious elite was not viewed as neutral arbiters between the 'haves' and 'have-nots'. In fact, the Church hierarchy was firmly part of the aristocracy, in power if not lineage, and as the incident at Leighlinbridge demonstrated, some sections of Anglo-Norman society viewed them with ill-concealed contempt.

## Christian Ideas

While Church leaders like Fitzjohn were busily ploughing the field where the reformation would eventually take root, this did not necessarily result in the populace losing faith in their religious beliefs. Indeed, the Christian beliefs of the people in medieval Ireland appeared resolute. In a world where literacy and education were limited to a small section of the population, Christianity was the way in which most understood and rationalised what could be a cruel and violent world. It also gave hope and belief in an afterlife, where even the meek could expect to enjoy a better life.

The presence of parish churches in every small town, village and hamlet helps in some way to explain the power of Christian ideas in medieval Europe. These churches were the centre of life for thousands of communities. From birth to death, much of daily life revolved around the church. Indeed, it was religious feast days that structured the year and gave people rest days, during which work was forbidden. The depth and power of Christian beliefs was particularly evident when those beliefs were perceived to be under threat.

In 1324, Arnold le Poer imprisoned Richard Ledrede, the Bishop of Ossory, over his role in the Alice Kyteler witchcraft trial (see chapter 13, p.87). In response, Ledrede placed the entire diocese of Ossory under interdict. This meant that Christianity – its rituals and spiritual protection – was effectively suspended: a frightening prospect for fourteenth-century Christians. In a diocese under interdiction, babies could not be baptised, the sick were refused anointment and the dead could not be buried in consecrated ground, all of which risked access to heaven and the fate of one's eternal soul.

Although Ledrede himself was austere, single-minded and fanatical about his beliefs, the community in Kilkenny rallied to his side. Crowds flocked to Kilkenny Castle where the bishop was imprisoned. Ledrede himself later described the scene: 'the people of the town were pouring up to the castle; they were paying much respect and great honour on the bishop, they were sending hundreds of presents to him, so the place looked more like a guest-house than a prison; everyone was flocking to receive his benediction'[77].

While the reaction of the people of Kilkenny to Ledrede's imprisonment stands in stark contrast to the reaction FitzJohn received in Leighlinbridge in 1305, Ledrede's decision to issue an interdiction may explain these conflicting responses. Dying under interdict endangered one's immortal soul. In a society where the majority firmly believed that they would spend eternity either in heaven or hell, such concerns were more than simply abstract, theological ideas.

In one respect, men like William FitzJohn, who had provoked such ire in Leighlinbridge, illustrated the strength of medieval Christianity: it was in spite of such disreputable representatives that Christian ideas held their power. The Church, however, was not immune from the problems and conflicts of wider society. Eventually, the conflict between the Gaelic Irish and the Anglo-Normans proved to be one of the greatest challenges to face the Church in the fourteenth century.

## Gaelic Irish Christianity vs Anglo-Norman Christianity

Almost immediately after the Anglo-Normans invaded Ireland, relations within the Church were placed under considerable strain. In 1172 the Gaelic Irish bishops met in a synod at Cashel and endorsed the conquest; this could not, however, alleviate the inevitable tensions. Over the following decades the Normans increasingly dominated positions of authority within the Church. This is demonstrated by the fact that after 1181 all of the archbishops in the diocese of Dublin were of Anglo-Norman descent. Many Anglo-Norman clerics held deeply bigoted views of the Gaelic Irish. One prominent Cistercian, Stephen of Lexington, referred to them as 'mere Irish'[78] and 'bestial'[79].

Lexington himself was involved in a vicious conflict that divided the Cistercians right up to the 1220s. Such was the depth of conflict that monks issued several death threats to each other! Eventually the Cistercian general chapter dealt with problematic houses, believed to be under the influence of Gaelic Irish clerics, by dispersing the Gaelic Cistercians to other monasteries. This was only the beginning, and the situation would deteriorate further.

By the late thirteenth century, as warfare between the colonists and the Gaelic Irish deepened, the clergy began to take sides. In 1299 the bishop of Kildare wrote to the king complaining of 'fanatic religious persons who were exciting disturbances and spreading in the Irish Language the seeds of rebellion'[80]. Likewise in 1317 Donal O'Neill, the Gaelic King of Tyrone, claimed in a letter to the Pope that a certain 'Friar Simon shamelessly burst out in words that it is no sin to kill a man of Irish birth'[81].

Such attitudes inevitably tested the faith of many Gaelic Irish, but many drew a distinction between these Anglo-Norman representatives of the Church and their personal Christian beliefs. There were others still, such as Adam Dubh O'Toole, who would go as far as rejecting many of the Church's core beliefs (see chapter 14, p.95).

# 6

# Women

In April 1312 William Frend appeared in court charged with killing Stephen Bray with an axe blow to the head. The murder had occurred during what might be considered a stereotypical medieval chivalric dispute: a quarrel over a woman's honour. While visiting their house, William's wife had asked Stephen Bray whether he would stay to dine with them. Inexplicably, Stephen not only refused, but then horribly insulted the woman calling her 'a hard woman and a vile'[82]. Not satisfied that he had insulted his host sufficiently, he went on to accuse her of being the mistress of the local priest. William Frend, outraged, would not allow the transgression to pass, and threw Stephen out of his house, proffering some insults of his own. Stephen retorted and threatened to strike 'William on the head till his brains gushed out'[83]. Hours later, thinking the issue had passed, Frend left his house on business, but, it being medieval Ireland, he armed himself with an axe.

The slighted Stephen Bray had, however, been waiting patiently for this moment. Seeing his opportunity, he lunged at William with an axe of his own. Unfortunately for the would-be murderer, he failed to countenance that his prey was himself armed, and the full gravity of his miscalculation soon revealed itself when Bray became the recipient of a fatal blow to the head[84]. While this may seem like any other story of violence from a violent world, it is also a revealing portrayal of how women in the medieval world were viewed. This event began with Stephen Bray insulting William Frend's wife. She, however, is completely passive in the record of events, a helpless individual whose honour needs to be protected by her husband; her name is not even mentioned. While it may snugly fit a stereotype, this is not a reflection of how medieval women lived their lives. Indeed, most were nothing like this stereotype. A story that portrays a very different view of medieval women's lives is that of Fyngole McTorkoill.

## Fyngole McTorkoill and the Escape from Dublin Castle

In July 1313 a gang of outlaws – Walter O Bryn, John McTorkoill, Thomas Ohenethan and Walter Conlyn – described as 'common robbers and notorious felons'[85], were captured and brought to Dublin Castle. There they were held, awaiting trial in the imposing fortress that formed the south-eastern corner of the medieval city. Imprisoned in dark and crowded cells, their prospects were poor. Almost certain to be convicted, their impending fate was the hangman's noose or worse. Helpless, all they could do was await their doom. However, outside the castle a woman called Fyngole McTorkoill was planning a gaol break. The night before their court case, she carried sheets into the castle, which were to be used by the prisoners to make cords, which they would use to climb down the castle walls. Unfortunately for all involved, they were caught. When they appeared before the Justiciar, two members of the gang were sentenced to hang while two others, their crimes being deemed to be of a more serious nature, received a particularly nasty punishment. They were humiliated and painfully tortured by being drawn behind the tails of horses through the streets of Dublin; only after this were they hanged.

Fyngole herself was also in trouble, having attempted to break them out. She was hauled before a court, but facing the highest official in the land she was by no means intimidated. Standing before Edmund Butler, the Justiciar, she pretended to be mute and refused to speak. Unfortunately, the jury didn't fall for the trick, and she was sent to prison and was eventually released.[86] While not many women (or men for that matter) engaged in such daring escapades, Fyngole's tale is an example of the many women who lived lives very different from the frequent stereotype of the meek medieval woman. Indeed, in the court sitting one month before Fyngole was sentenced, another woman called Lucia was in court having been arrested on suspicion of being involved in a robbery. She and another thief were accused of waylaying Andrew Gerrard before robbing him of twenty marks, a very large sum of money at the time.[87]

## Women's Lives in Medieval Ireland

While there was no universal female experience of the medieval world, it is fair to say that life for many women was often a struggle. Their interaction with power and authorities was very different to that of men. They lived in a deeply sexist world that viewed them as naturally incapable and illogical. If the late medieval period had opinion-shapers, then thirteenth-century theologian St Thomas Aquinas was certainly one. Aquinas outlined what was probably the prevailing view of women: 'Woman is naturally subject to man because in man the discretion of reason predominates'[88].

In order to achieve even limited independence, women had to struggle constantly; they held few rights or privileges. Married women were legally subject to their husband, while life for single women was very difficult, especially for the poor, who struggled to survive. For example, in the summer of 1343 the Priory of the Holy Trinity in Dublin hired a thatcher to re-roof the barns and stables on their farms. To aid with the work they hired a serving man to carry up mud and straw to the thatcher. They also hired two women to draw the straw and carry water. The thatcher was paid one penny per day with food, the serving man was given one penny per day without food, while the two women were paid only a half-penny per day with no mention of meals.[89]

Towns and cities did offer women greater opportunities. In urban environments they appear to have been able to find independence easier, most notably in the brewing trade.[90] Indeed, when the 'laws and usages' of Dublin were drawn up in the fourteenth century, it appears brewing was exclusively run by women, all laws and regulations referring to 'woman brewers'[91]. To what extent women engaged in business on a wider level is hard to tell, but there is some evidence that they could rise high in urban society.[92] Alice Kyteler, who gained fame when she was accused of witchcraft in 1324 (see chapter 13, p. 87), was a merchant and banker in Kilkenny with considerable power and influence. This is not to imply, of course, that towns were a haven of equality. While women were afforded opportunities, this did not mean they did not face other constraints. One law stipulated that 'every woman retailer, sitting in the street with a basket, for the week'[93] was to be charged a farthing to aid with the cleaning of the street. This implies that many women were unable to afford shops, and basically hawked goods on the streets.

## Roesia de Verdun

Against overwhelming odds, some women did succeed in rising to the highest levels of medieval society. One of the most famous women in Norman Ireland was Isybel de Clare, daughter of the man who spearheaded the conquest of Ireland, Richard de Clare, and better known as Strongbow. Isybel married William Marshall, one of the most famous figures of the thirteenth century, who was involved in many key events of the medieval era from the Crusades to the Magna Carta. Isybel not only exerted huge influence through her high-ranking husband, but was respected in her own right. She was the only woman recorded as an official witness to a business transaction in the thousands of documents preserved in the Ormond Deeds[94]. Successful as Isybel was, the most powerful woman in medieval Irish history was unquestionably Roesia de Verdun, although like all other women she had to fight to be recognised in the world in which she lived.

Roesia was born c. 1204 into a wealthy and powerful noble family with large estates in England, Wales and Ireland. She was named after her grandmother who died in January 1215 while Roesia was still a child. Although little is known of Roesia de Verdun's teenage years, she was married to a husband who died by the time she reached her twenties and there appear to have been no surviving children. As her father, Nicolas de Verdun, had no sons either, Roesia found herself heiress to the large de Verdun estates, and soon she was faced with the prospect of remarriage. In 1225 King Henry III wrote to her father instructing him to remarry Roesia to a powerful noble Theobald Walter (Butler). This was quite literally a medieval offer Nicolas could not refuse, and later in the year Roesia was wed to Walter. That she was twice married at a relatively young age was by no means unusual. High mortality rates often made two or even three marriages in a lifetime quite common.

In the following years she gave birth to her only known surviving child, John. Her husband Theobald died when fighting for King Henry III in Poitou, France in 1230, and the following year everything changed dramatically when the other significant male figure in her life, her father, died. As his only heir, Roesia became one of the major landowners in the Anglo-Norman colony of Ireland. While she also inherited vast family estates in England, her most troublesome lands were those in Ireland. Centred in modern County Louth, she not only faced a difficult challenge from the Gaelic Irish from whom the lands had been stolen a few decades previously, but also surrounding Norman lords. Since the Norman colony's inception in the 1170s it had been riven with infighting between various powerful factions, which resulted in violent disputes. In this environment, and with no male heir to rule her estates, the surrounding noble families hovered like vultures around what they perceived as easy targets, with potentially devastating results. There were few tactics that power-hungry Norman Lords in such situations would not use for their own benefit. In 1305 the Lord of Offaly John Fitzthomas repeatedly spread rumours that the recently widowed Agnes de Valance had died as a ruse for him to take her lands forcibly.[95] When Walter de Burgh, the Earl of Ulster, died in 1271, his heir Richard was only twelve. For the following decade his widow Aveline de Burgh struggled to hold family territories together as a civil war broke out across Ulster. It was into this world that Roesia de Verdun to enter in the years following her father's death.

To the north of her lands lay the Earldom of Ulster, ruled by the predatory individual Hugh de Lacy. De Lacy had effectively conquered Ulster by military force from

the previous Earl John de Courcy in an invasion in 1204.
Worse still, de Lacy had a claim on Roesia's lands, having
married her aunt Lecelina. Given the chance, he would
attempt to take her estates, by force if necessary.

One solution open to women faced with such a
predicament was to marry a powerful noble. If Roesia
had done so, this would have given her access to increased
military might to defend her lands. Nevertheless, having
spent her late teens and early twenties in medieval
marriages, Roesia had little desire to marry for a third time
and rejected the societal pressure to do so. Unfortunately,
King Henry III was another matter entirely, and it was he
who ultimately wielded control over whether she would
marry again. Regardless, she persevered, and in October
1231, when she paid the large sum of 700 marks to inherit
her father's lands, she also bought the rights to her marriage
and included the clause 'she may not be constrained to
marry' in this agreement with the king. Having secured
control over her own destiny, or as much control as was
possible in feudal society, she turned to the defence of her
holdings in Ireland. Defying convention, in the following
years Roesia invested huge energy into developing these
lands. In 1235 she successfully ended the greatest Norman
threat to her Irish estates when she came to an agreement
with her uncle-in-law Hugh de Lacy. They agreed a deal
in which he finally relinquished claims he had on the de
Verdun lands in Louth. In the following years Roesia moved
to defend the lands from the Gaelic Irish. After obtaining
permission in 1237, she constructed a massive fortification,
Castleroche, near Dundalk; a feat that the king noted
'none of her predecessors was able to do'[96]. This is the only
known case of a woman raising a castle in medieval Irish
history. Despite these great accomplishments it appears that
even a woman as confident and powerful as Roesia could

only resist societal pressures to remarry for so long. Facing increased insistence she would not relent, and in 1242 she retired to a monastery, which she founded in Leicester.[97] In the following years, as her son took the reins of power, she faded into obscurity before her incredible life finally came to a close in 1247.

In achieving her successes, Roesia obviously benefited from her high birth. For most women in medieval Ireland such power was out of reach, not just because they were women, but because they were poor; theirs was a struggle merely to survive. Nevertheless, the achievements of Roesia de Verdun were undoubtedly remarkable. Her success was illustrated when her son John took her surname rather than the surname of his father Theobald Walter (Butler), while her actions secured the position of the de Verdun family as one of the preeminent Norman families in Ireland.

# 7

# Mob Rule:
# Protest in Medieval Ireland

In February 1310, the leading figures of Norman Ireland gathered to attend Parliament in Kilkenny. The Normans faced a mounting crisis as the Gaelic Irish attacked the colony with increasing success. To make matters worse, the colonial aristocrats had become a law unto themselves. In Kilkenny, the Parliament heard how 'merchants and the common part of the people of this land are impoverished and oppressed by prises of the great lords of the land who take what they will through the country'[98]. Merchants and common people, however, were not going to find succour from resolutions passed by the Parliament gathered in Kilkenny in 1310. The gathering was dominated by the same 'great lords' who were in fact the cause of such distress and hardship.

Parliaments in the Middle Ages were not democratic institutions. Attendees at Parliament were not elected; rather, they were an elite group, hand-picked by the king. Prior to the meeting in Kilkenny, Edward II summoned over 100 members of the aristocracy; the senior clergy; the merchant elite; royal officials and representatives from every town or borough in the Anglo-Norman colony – these were all men with extensive wealth and property. Given that those who suffered most under this regime were not represented at Parliament, it is of little surprise that the resolutions passed there bore little consequence to the lives of ordinary people. The aristocracy had no intention of curbing their behaviour; indeed, it failed to resolve any of the major issues facing Ireland in 1310.

Peasants, the overwhelming bulk of the population, had no representation in Parliament at all. Their counterparts in towns and cities did not fare much better. Even though there were two representatives from each town, most urban dwellers still had no say. A significant minority in towns had the privilege of citizenship of their settlements. This allowed them to elect mayors and officials, but nonetheless urban life in medieval Ireland was dominated by small groups of powerful families. Between 1302 and 1322, just seven men held the annually elected position of Mayor of Dublin. A similar situation prevailed in Kilkenny. Between 1293 and 1323, the position of Mayor of Kilkenny was held by members of only nine prominent families.

These urban elites also had strong links to the nobility: the one-time Mayor of Dublin, Geoffrey Morton, worked as a representative for the Earl of Ulster[99], while another mayor, William Douce, represented Piers de Bermingham, the Lord of Tethmoy[100]. These merchant elites were unlikely to force meaningful change from the nobility. During the Middle Ages, numerous and often life-threatening problems faced many, and protest was one of the few avenues open to those excluded from public life.

## Rural Revolt

One of the largest groups in society, with some of the greatest grievances, consisted of poorer peasants and labourers.

Living on and working lands owned by the nobility, they worked according to agreements that were often bound by time-honoured custom. Many did not even enjoy basic freedom of movement without the express permission of their lord. This restriction prevented peasants and labourers from seeking improved conditions elsewhere. In 1299, with labour supply in high demand, the peasants were presented with a rare opportunity to improve their living standards.

In the final year of the thirteenth century, Anglo-Norman Ireland was emerging from one of the most difficult periods since the invasion of the previous century. In 1295 a horrific famine had devastated Ireland. The Annals of Inisfallen recorded the devastation in the following manner: 'very stormy weather this year, with wind, snow, and lightning, and a great murrain of cattle and loss of life also'[101]. To make matters worse, something approaching a civil war broke out between the Lord of Offaly and the Earl of Ulster, destroying much property. Although it is impossible to tell exactly how many died during this period of war and starvation, the poor suffered disproportionately, as food prices increased dramatically (see chapter 4, p.37).

By 1299 the crisis had passed. Indeed, that year there was a great harvest, which was reflected in the collapse of wheat prices to two shillings a crannock (approximately half the normal price). Given the previous years of famine and war, the available workforce to gather the crops had been significantly reduced. Such circumstances presented the poor with an opportunity. Reports came in from around 'diverse communities and counties' in Ireland that 'servants, ploughmen, carters, threshers, and other their servants refuse to serve ... for which they are accustomed to serve'[102]. This report marks one of the earliest recorded strikes in Ireland, and posed a major threat to feudal society.

Central to the feudal system was the practice of peasants and labourers being bound by custom and tradition, regardless of wider living conditions.

On 3 May 3 1299, Parliament was convened in Dublin. The nobility was keen to reassert its authority. They declared that servants were bound to accept the dues and wages of previous years. It appears, however, that some nobles, desperate for labour, were willing to break ranks and offer better conditions, leading Parliament to decree: 'Nor is it permitted to anyone to draw away or keep a servant or maid of his neighbour or of another, without the will of him with whom he stayed before'[103]. After this parliamentary session there are no further surviving records of unrest. Given that sheriffs were instructed to imprison anyone who defied the law, it seems that the labourers' protests may have been defeated on this occasion.

Twenty years later a similar situation arose. Between 1315 and 1318 over 10% of the population perished as a result of war and famine (see chapter 4, p.37). While there is little evidence of widespread demands for increased wages as occurred in 1299, there is anecdotal evidence suggesting that some peasants successfully forced lords to reduce rents. In 1326, the Archbishop of Dublin was offering land for no rent, save one day's labour[104].

It was not until 1349, following one the darkest chapters in human history, that the tide turned against the nobility. In the aftermath of the Black Death there was a chronic labour shortage; between the harvests of 1348 and 1349, it is estimated that up to half the workforce had died. For those who survived 'the Great Mortality' the balance of power shifted, at least momentarily, as the labour shortage created opportunities for labourers to demand higher wages and improved conditions.

Having survived what must at times have seemed like the end of days, labourers now realised their power. Many were unwilling to return to a life of servitude, which had been a hallmark of their existence. Instead, they demanded higher wages, and often voted with their feet if the lord did not accede to their demands. With such a shortage of labour supply, they could now seek better remuneration elsewhere.

In an effort to stem this growing unrest, the king introduced a new law in 1349. It decreed that labourers must return to work for rates that had existed before the plague of 1346. However, this attempt to turn the clock back was wishful thinking on the Crown's part. The poor were not only were in a dominant position due to the dramatic population decline, but they were also driven to improve the harsh conditions they experienced in post–Black Death Ireland. In the aftermath of the plague, food was scarce, which resulted in increased prices[105], and consequently higher wages were demanded.

Unsurprisingly, the laws introduced were not successful, and had to be reissued and expanded under the Statute of Labourers in 1351. This statute restricted the movement of peasants, as well as their wages and other forms of remuneration. It resulted in a bitter struggle in many areas as peasants continued to defy the authorities and to seek better conditions. Unfortunately, no court records survive in Ireland from this period, and so there are no accounts of peasants resisting these laws. Records from England, however, provide a glimpse of what may have been happening in Ireland at the same time.

In 1352, John Boltash, carter of the local parson in Wroughton, Wiltshire pleaded guilty to receiving two bushels of wheat for ten weeks' work, when he was accustomed to receive one bushel for eleven weeks of work[106]. Others simply left service regardless of previous agreements. Edward le Taillour made an agreement to work for the convent of Bradenstoke, Wiltshire for a year from September 1351. By December, however, le Taillour no longer wanted to stay, perhaps having been offered better conditions elsewhere. Without permission, he simply left[107]; a dramatic response, given the servile lives labourers had once been forced to live. All the authorities could do was instruct the bailiff to arrest him. This was a tough task, given that le Taillour was by no means the only labourer on the move. It is likely that similar situations prevailed in Ireland. In Kilkenny the town authorities entered the 1349 law, prohibiting increased wages and conditions, into the Liber Primus (the official written record of city life), indicating that the issue of wages may have been of particular relevance at that time.

These laws, however, failed to force a return to pre-plague working conditions. Throughout the later fourteenth century many similar statutes were enacted, indicating that they had limited impact in stemming wages and the movement of labour. While such peasant protest is the most well-known form of dissent during the medieval period, the peasantry was by no means alone in taking a stand over its grievances.

## Nobility vs Towns

Alongside the protests of the rural poor, the nobility also incurred the wrath of the townspeople. A major source of tension was the actions of feudal lords and their armed retinues. The 1310, Parliament noted that 'merchants and others passing through the country are robbed of their goods by those of great lineage'[108]. Their deprivations were not limited to rural areas, as Parliament continued: 'such malefactors take, as well in towns ... without making reasonable payment'[109]. Indeed, the situation had become so serious that merchants began avoiding parts of the colony. Often townspeople had little option but to oppose the nobles directly themselves; the royal authorities were of little use. The chief royal official in Ireland, the Justiciar, was often one of the same nobles they had issue with.

Evidence of the tensions that existed is provided by the failed attempt of Piers de Bermingham, Lord of Tethmoy, and his army to gain entry to the town of Drogheda in 1305. De Bermingham was on his way to fight for the king in Scotland, but regardless of his mission, the people of Drogheda refused to allow his army into the town. When the soldiers attempted to forcibly gain entry, three troops were killed by the townspeople. In the aftermath of the fracas the soldiers were banned from the town, while merchants were forbidden to sell them food or supplies. It was further decreed that if any of de Bermingham's men entered the town they would be imprisoned. When five soldiers subsequently made an attempt to enter Drogheda, they were attacked, beaten, imprisoned and held for two days.[110] These actions eventually forced de Bermingham to move on, saving the town from the lawlessness of his soldiers. This was by no means an isolated incident. Similar grievances provoked conflict in Dublin during the Bruce Invasion of 1315, when tensions between the nobility and the inhabitants of the city reached breaking-point.

In the months following the arrival of an invading army led by Edward Bruce, brother of the King of Scotland, Dublin city and the surrounding region suffered greatly. It was not the Scots who caused this damage, however, but the armies of the Anglo-Norman nobles, raised to defend the Anglo-Norman colony. As they passed through Dublin, en route to Ulster to fight the Scots, they appear to have gone on the rampage. The damage was so extensive that the king granted a remission of rent of £60 per annum for four years to the people of Dublin 'in consideration of losses entailed on the citizens [of Dublin] by concourse of armed men marching towards Ulster against the Scots; the destruction of the greater part of the suburbs of the city; and the decrease of revenue'[111]. This dramatically heightened tensions between the city and the nobility. In early 1317 these tensions erupted when the Dublin was besieged by a large Scots army.

In February, a large Scots force, led by the King of Scotland himself, Robert the Bruce, bore down on the city. The only major noble in the city at the time was Richard de Burgh, the Earl of Ulster, who was the most powerful aristocrat in Ireland. Having been crushed by Edward Bruce at the Battle of Connor in 1315, however, de Burgh had no army with which to defend the city. He and a small retinue quartered themselves in St Mary's Abbey, just across the river from the city walls, but he soon became the focus of popular anger in a town facing siege. Not only was de Burgh a member of the class that had caused so much grief for Dublin; he had also long been the subject of ill-founded rumours that he was in league with the Scots.

Although the rumours were untrue, the fact that de Burgh was Robert the Bruce's father-in-law fuelled speculation. This rumour and the long-running tensions between the nobility and the city pushed the inhabitants of Dublin to act against de Burgh. With the Scots bearing down on the city, the mayor, Robert de Nottingham, led a mob of Dubliners to the Abbey and demanded that de Burgh be handed over. When the request was refused, the mob killed seven members of de Burgh's retinue and eventually set fire to the earl's quarters in an attempt to force him out. He was arrested and imprisoned in Dublin Castle. While the city was successfully defended, de Burgh was not released. Instead he was held for several months, exacerbating tensions with the aristocracy still further.

When Parliament was summoned in Dublin later in 1317, the king was forced to give explicit instructions to hold the gathering in a place outside Dublin due to tensions between the nobility and the citizens[112]. The gravity of the situation led Edward II to decree that no 'parliaments or assemblies to be held in the city during the existence of these dissensions, nor to permit the magnates or their men to be housed within the city against the will of the community'[113].

## The Common Folk of Dublin

Worn down by several years of war, the city of Dublin appears to have been in full revolt. Not only were there tensions between the city and the aristocracy, there was also widespread conflict between the inhabitants themselves. Around this time those termed the 'common folk' were seriously aggrieved by what they called 'the inefficient government of the city rulers'[114]. They drew up a manifesto of sorts, containing twenty-one demands, and sent it to the king. While some of the demands focussed on equitable and fair taxation, many reflected grievances relating to the city's recent experiences of war and famine. The 'common folk' demanded that the standard of bread in the city be maintained at a decent level and that quality tests be carried more frequently.[115] Severe sanctions were also demanded against 'regraters' – middlemen who profiteered in the food markets, thereby pushing the price of food upwards.[116] On the issue of defence of the city, they called for a heightened level of civic duty. The manifesto implored that when called on, at least one person would come from each house to defend the city against 'Scotch enemies, and by the hostile Irish who daily threaten to burn the suburb and to do all possible damage to the city'[117].

These demands appear to have been directed at the city rulers, who in the early fourteenth century were a clique of rich merchants, notorious for their abuse of power. A few years previously, one-time Lord Mayor Geoffrey Morton was convicted of corrupt practices dating back to 1311. The fact that the sitting mayor, Robert de Nottingham, was Morton's former son-in-law did little to help build confidence in the city's political elite. These protests within the city may even explain why de Nottingham was willing, taking what might seem to have been an unusual stand, to lead the attack on the Earl of Ulster in St Mary's Abbey in February 1317. What became of the demands is unclear, but tensions in Dublin rumbled on for decades, particularly between the city and royal officials. By 1323 the citizens of Dublin were again up in arms, as the Justiciar and his officials used the houses of the city inhabitants as quarters and appropriated their property.[118]

Protest is often considered a modern phenomenon, developing alongside the evolution of democracy. This is not the case. It was immensely important part of life in medieval Ireland. Having been frozen out of the power structure, it was the only way many could force the aristocracy or merchants to curb the worst excesses of their behaviour. Often such protests were literally a matter of life and death for the poor.

# 8

# Grub's up!
# Food in Medieval Ireland

During summers of plenty, late medieval Ireland was a land abundant with food. In good years, fields swayed with great crops of wheat, oats, corn and barley. Shepherds tended to large flocks and herds of animals, which were reared for meat and dairy products. The sheer size of these animal herds was staggering; in 1290 alone, 51,000 cattle hides were exported from Irish ports.[119] Milk from both cows and sheep was converted into cheese and butter while rabbits, swans, peacocks and hens were also commonly reared for the dinner table.[120]

A wide variety of vegetables were grown including onions, garlic, leek and kale. While the countryside supplied many staples of the medieval diet, an even wider variety of foods was available for purchase in urban markets. The numerous coastal towns attracted fishermen, who brought ashore large stocks of fish; salmon and eel were particularly popular. When not consumed immediately, fish was preserved through salting so it could be exported. While pigs were common in the countryside, they were also a feature of everyday life in both towns and cities. Indeed, they were a constant nuisance in urban environments, and their owners were subject to laws to keep them under control.[121] Once slaughtered, pigs were eaten as pork or salted for bacon.

It was at the docks of port towns that some of the most unusual foods arrived in Ireland. Far from the banal diet we might expect, delicacies were imported in large quantities. Wine and salt arrived from western France. Rice grown in the Mediterranean Basin was eaten in Dublin, frequently flavoured with almond milk. There were also even more exotic goods to be found. Ginger, pepper, cinnamon and cloves were imported from Asia and available in fourteenth-century Ireland.

While the food markets of medieval Dublin could whet even the modern appetite, most people who lived in the city never experienced the more exotic and tasty foods. A person's access to wealth and their status in medieval society determined their diet.

## The Diets of the Rich and Poor

The sharp contrast in the differing foods various social classes ate can be seen when we look at the diet of two contemporaries from the period. The first, Gilbert de Bolyniop, was a member of the elite of medieval society in Ireland. Gilbert was prior of one of the richest religious foundations in Dublin: the Priory of the Holy Trinity, better known today as Christchurch, between 1337 and 1343. As prior he was one of the most important figures in medieval Ireland. He frequently attended, and on occasion hosted, meetings of the medieval Parliament. He also had access to great wealth, as he ruled over one of the oldest religious institutions in Dublin.

At the other end of the medieval spectrum was a man called Robert le Dryvere. Robert lived on the prior's lands in Grangegorman, which was situated just outside Oxmantown, the northern suburb of medieval Dublin. Robert worked as a driver of a plough team; his name le Dryvere derived from his work[122]. His meagre annual salary came to sixty pence, which in 1343 was supplemented by an extra four pence. His greatest single outlay was the rent for the cottage he held from the priory, which cost him twelve pence per year. While Robert was by no means the poorest in medieval Dublin, he nonetheless lived in an entirely different world than prior Gilbert. This contrast was starkly obvious in what they ate.

Gilbert could afford whatever foods took his fancy, and the delicacies of Dublin's food markets were at his disposal. From surviving priory accounts we know that on a Thursday in Lent 1338, Gilbert was joined by Hugh de Saltu (a canon from the nearby St Patrick's Cathedral) among others for dinner. As it was Lent, the ecclesiastics could not eat meat, but nonetheless they enjoyed a sumptuous meal that included bread, wine, ale, herrings, turbot, plaice and trout, all of which cost just over twenty-five pence. For desert they supped on rice in almond milk, the rice and almonds costing a further four pence[123]. This one meal alone cost nearly half of Robert le Dryvere's annual salary.

Spending four pence on rice and almonds was a luxury, but this was by no means the only extravagance the prior enjoyed. He also ate foods flavoured by ginger, saffron[124] and olive oil[125]. On another occasion he dined on imported figs[126]. When not constrained by Lenten prohibition, the prior enjoyed fine meals of meat. In early 1338 on the feast of St Agnes the Virgin, he ate with the proctors John Welsh and Walter Brayhenogh. They enjoyed a meal of two cooked capons, which are roosters castrated when young; a mutilation that produces succulent meat. These were accompanied by other assorted roast meats, which all cost eleven pence. On other days he enjoyed pasties, pies, roasted fowl and salted eels.

This diet was by no means limited just to one lavish prior. Similar accounts are recorded in the satirical poem 'The land of Cockayne', written in the fourteenth century, most likely by an anonymous Franciscan.[127] The author attacked the lavishness of a neighbouring religious house of the wealthy Cistercian Order. In the satire he mentions numerous dishes enjoyed by Cistercians, which included larks cooked in cinnamon and cloves, and geese cooked in garlic.[128]

While such meals are mouth-watering to say the least, the majority of the population of medieval Dublin could never afford such gastronomic delights. Robert le Dryvere, the poor ploughman who lived on the Prior's lands, could afford very little of the food from the prior's table. Indeed, of the delightful fish dinner the prior hosted during Lent 1338, the onions used to flavour the food was probably the only item on the menu that Robert could have afforded. Onions were relatively cheap at two pence for half a stone[129]. This was due to the fact that they could be easily grown in the surrounding countryside or even in the city gardens.

Robert and those like him, the poor of medieval society, lived primarily on a diet of a stew–like substance called pottage, eaten with bread. Pottage was in essence a vegetable stew made from peas, beans, onions, leaks and kale, and then flavoured with herbs. The staple of later Irish peasants, the potato, would not be introduced for centuries, well after the European conquest of the Americas begun in 1492.

Living on pottage, medieval peasants were in effect vegetarians most of the time. This was not by choice; meat was generally far too expensive. Alongside pottage, the poor would have eaten bread, but even with this most simple of foods, the rich and poor dined differently. People like Robert could have rarely afforded bread made from wheat, but instead ate cheaper breads made from corn and rye. Such bread, baked from poorly sieved flour had serious long-term health ramifications for the poor of medieval Ireland.

The bread frequently contained grit from millstones as it was poorly sieved. Chewing this grit-laden bread had a detrimental impact on teeth, and indeed on wider health. The skulls of human remains found in excavations from thirteenth- and fourteenth-century Dublin revealed extremely worn teeth, to such an extent that the dental pulp had been exposed.[130] This would have resulted in excruciatingly painful infections and abscesses. Such afflictions would have affected the elite to a much lesser degree; they enjoyed bread that was far better in quality. On occasion, prior Gilbert ate pandemain; a very expensive bread made from wheat flour that had been sifted several times.

## Lethal Takeaways

While Robert's diet paled in contrast to what prior Gilbert enjoyed, there were those in a worse position. In order to make even the most basic meals like pottage, a person required a home with kitchen implements and a large pot. Many, however, did not even possess these basics. According to Alexander de Bicknor, the Archbishop of Dublin who reigned between 1317 and 1349, the city of Dublin and its suburbs were infested by 'stragglers and beggars'[131] in the fourteenth century. Such people were dependent on pre-cooked foods like bread and ale. In medieval towns, takeaway food of this kind could be very dangerous.

Judging by contemporary accounts from medieval London, the urban poor who purchased cooked food that was sold in the streets frequently risked their lives in doing so. The food appears to have been of a very poor quality. The great poet of the age, Geoffrey Chaucer, described a pie shop in his work *The Canterbury Tales* as fly-infested and the source of reheated, soggy pies. In the other great epic of the era, *The Vision of Piers Plowman*, William Langland relates how the brewers, bakers, butchers and cooks frequently poisoned the poor of London through bad produce. It would appear that the same problem prevailed in Ireland.

In Kilkenny, laws and ordinances that date from the later fourteenth century specifically mention a punishment for cooks 'who boil meat or fish in bread or water or in any other way not fit for human consumption'[132] (the mention of cooking meat in bread is presumably a reference to pies). There is also specific reference to those who sell foods after they 'lose their nature and reheat them and sell them'.[133]

Similarly, in the laws and usages of Dublin, which date from the early fourteenth century, regulations were introduced by which bakers could be fined for producing 'faulty bread'[134]. Punishments against brewers who made poor quality ale were also common. In Kilkenny, for example, they faced a fine of fifteen pence for making inferior ale.[135] No matter what risk medieval brewers posed to their clients, it was a far safer option than drinking water from public water sources in the city. In 1337 in Kilkenny, a law was enacted punishing people for washing their clothes or animal intestines in public fountains.[136]

Food in the medieval era was as highly segregated as the society itself. People like Robert le Dryvere and the 'stragglers and beggars' of medieval Dublin had as much chance of eating most of the foodstuffs to be found on the archbishop's table as they did of sitting at that table. They were consigned to eating what was available to them. Some, like Robert, could live relatively healthy lives on pottage as long as there were not food shortages; those at the very bottom of society, however, ran a gauntlet every day by risking the cooked food on medieval city streets.

# 9

# In Sickness and in Health

T repanation is a bone-chilling procedure. It involves cutting back the skin of the scalp before using a circular saw to carve through the bone of the human skull. This operation, practised in Europe for millennia[137] without anaesthetic, was an extremely painful and uncomfortable procedure. While trepanation has long had associations with supernatural beliefs, it was also performed for therapeutic reasons in medieval Ireland. A skull found in an excavation from medieval Dublin (which could not be dated to a specific century) bore the distinct marks of a trepanation carried out to alleviate suffering from a skull fracture. A sub-circular piece of bone measuring roughly two centimetres in diameter had been removed, but unfortunately the patient died shortly after the operation; there was no evidence of healing.[138] Many who endured the operation didn't die after the procedure; several skulls with trepanation marks show evidence of healing around the wound.

This highly advanced technique, even without the aid of anaesthetic and scans, sheds a different light on what is often considered the basic and barbaric field of medieval medicine. However, it is only part of the story of health and healthcare in the later Middle Ages. There are also numerous examples of how people failed to comprehend even the most basic of medical problems. Indeed, this inability to grapple with some basic illnesses may be the root of some of more zany accounts that survive from medieval Ireland – accounts that at times appear outlandish. Some are disturbingly naïve given that these are the same people who attempted to carve human skulls open.

In 1341 one annalist in Dublin reported that there:

> ... chanced in the county of Leicester a strange thing; where there was a certain man going in the open street found a pair of gloves as he thought fit for his purpose which he put upon his hands and suddenly in that place did lose his speech and wonderfully did yole and cry like a dog which infected in that country as well old as young, that made noise some like big dog and some like small cats which infirmity continued with some very long, and some a month and with some others two month.[139]

Unquestionably, this is a bizarre story. Ultimately we will never know exactly what the annalist was referring to, given the passage of time past. While it is possible that the annalist was enjoying particularly strong ale, it is unlikely that these events were not without some basis. The original source (the annals kept at the Cistercian Abbey of St Mary's in Dublin) is generally quite reliable. While the stories of the glove being the cause of the incident are clearly added for dramatic purposes, the core of the story may not be as fantastical as it sounds. The yowling and crying like a dog may well be an attempt to explain a medical condition, perhaps pertussis (commonly known as whooping cough) which is often described as a barking like sound. If the basis of this story was an attempt to explain an illness, it was by no means unique; for every skilled surgeon who could perform trepanations, there were countless others who could offer fantastical and sometimes ludicrous explanations for illnesses. Many stemmed from the fact that there was very little understanding of anatomy and physiology.

The key concept that dominated medical thought was based around the theory of miasmatic transmission of disease. This held that disease passed from person to person, not through the transmission of bacteria or viruses, but through a vague notion of corrupted air, and to a lesser extent corrupted water. This concept led to cures that seem bizarre to us today given our understanding of disease. One of the most common remedies for illness was the practice of bloodletting. This frequently only served to weaken a gravely ill patient still further.

## Religious Ideas

Religion was a driving force in all aspects of medieval life, and medicine was not exempt. In what was a deeply fatalistic world view, many held that a vengeful God had a hand in sickness as a punishment for human bad behaviour. Following on from this, they argued that prayer was the solution. One such believer was the fanatical Bishop of Ossory, Richard Ledrede, who proclaimed:

> ... *the wound of Christ's side is the medicine above all others...*
> *for the fevered, the chilled, the withered, the dropsical, cripples,*
> *paralytics, the broken limbed, the swollen,*

> *Lepers, demoniacs, the desperate, the dead — it cures every ill*[140]

In short, he believed there was nothing another Mass couldn't cure. Ultimately, no one in the medieval world had an accurate understanding of what caused illness or how to cure it. While there were remedies for some illnesses, there was often no understanding as to why they were effective. In this environment it is hardly surprising that medieval Ireland was ravaged by deadly diseases, several of which are understood and controlled today.

In the centuries prior to the 1340s, one of the most well-known diseases was leprosy. In the twelfth and thirteenth centuries it was responsible for around 1% of deaths.[141] Despite its drastic effects, there was little or no treatment available. It was not exclusively a disease of the poor and underprivileged; leprosy even carried away the rich and powerful. Among the more famous victims were Baldwin IV, King of Jerusalem, who died in 1185, and possibly Robert the Bruce, King of Scotland, who died in 1329.

The only effective way to control the spread of the disease was to exclude sufferers from society. This was ritualised through a religious service that effectively condemned them to a life as a social pariah. The final line ominously stated: 'Be thou dead to the world, but alive again unto God'.[142] After this, they were confined to leper hospitals for the rest of their lives. There were several such leper hospitals in Ireland, purpose-built after the Norman Conquest.

The port of Waterford constructed the first leper hospital in the late twelfth century, while Dublin had at least two by the end of the thirteenth century. By the 1300s there were dozens spread across the island. Even smaller towns like Claregalway in the west of Ireland and

Gowran in the Nore Valley required such institutions. The trace of these hospitals can be seen across the landscape today in the place names: St Stephen's, Leperstown, Lazar and Maudlin, all of which usually denote the presence of a leper hospital.

## Plague

While leprosy was a brutal disease, and society's treatment was harsh on both the sufferer and their relations, worse was to come. Armed with their misinformed medical ideas, they faced the greatest recorded medical disaster in human history. This was Yersinia Pestis, commonly known as the Black Death. Named 'The Great Mortality' by contemporaries, its presence was first recorded in Europe in the port of Caffa on the Black Sea in 1347. Within a two-year period it had reached every corner of the continent, moving at such speed that even modern science would have struggled to curb its progress. Needless to say, medieval medics were completely out of their depth. The isolation treatment that had worked to contain leprosy for centuries was not feasible on a large scale, considering that over half the population was affected.

In an attempt to stem the spread of disease, King Philip VI of France appointed the leading scholars in Europe at the University of Paris to investigate the illness. Their leading theory was that the plague had ultimately been caused by corrupted airs. The folly of contemporary medical thought was demonstrated when they proclaimed the underlying reason to be a planetary alignment of Saturn, Jupiter and Mars at 1.00 p.m. on 20 March 1345.[143] The only effective remedy people found was to flee towns and cities where the disease ran riot. Pope Clement VI survived by fleeing the papal court at Avignon, which was devastated by the disease.

Unsurprisingly, as medicine was unable to cope, some turned to religion, which proved equally ineffective. Rejecting conventional religious institutions, as it became clear they could not provide a cure, some turned to extremism to beg forgiveness from what they saw as the acts of a vengeful God. In continental Europe there were cases of pogroms against Jews after rumours abounded that they were responsible for the plague. The Flagellant movement was another extreme reaction to the plague, which saw participants roam the countryside performing rituals, the most extreme of which saw severe self-flagellation or whipping to atone for their supposed sins. Such extreme responses appear to have been limited or non-existent in Ireland. There were no pogroms against Jews, as there was no Jewish community to speak of in medieval Ireland. Needless to say, all religious solutions proved to be as ineffectual as medieval medicine, but not everyone suffered equally.

## Life Expectancy

The Black Death, and indeed all illnesses in medieval Ireland, was not an equal-opportunity killer. The poor lived unhealthy lives and suffered illness far more than the rich. Disparity in general health was starkly obvious when we look at life expectancy, which archaeologists have been able to accurately estimate from the analysis of human remains. A survey of skeletons found in County Cork revealed staggering figures. One quarter of the population died before their early twenties, while in the following ten years a further 35% died.[144] While there are fluctuations in the exact details, these figures tally with other data from across the medieval world; over 50% of the population died before they reached their thirtieth birthday. While these numbers are general figures across society, historical accounts indicate that there were an elite few who lived far longer.

In 1314 Geoffrey de Geneville, the one-time Lord of Trim and in later years a Franciscan friar, was eighty-eight when he died. His wife Maud predeceased him by only twelve years, having lived until at least her seventies; the two had been married in 1252 and Maud was already a widow. While the de Genevilles lived exceptionally long lives, many of their aristocratic contemporaries also outlived most people. Richard de Burgh, the Earl of Ulster, lived to the grand old age of sixty-seven, while the average age of the five kings who ruled England between 1199 and 1375 was fifty-eight. It is no coincidence that these people came from the same aristocratic class in society, who lived for twice as long as most of those who worked their lands. This was primarily due to their living conditions.

Throughout the medieval period the aristocracy lived far healthier lives than their peasant counterparts. They for the most part lived in large, spacious castles. By the thirteenth century they increasingly had their own private chambers where they slept in dry and, as much as was possible, warm quarters. Increasingly during the thirteenth century, castles were serviced by garderobes, which carried human waste away; a major advancement in health. The diet of aristocrats (see chapter 8, p. 59) was almost incomparable, and they rarely, if ever, starved. They did not have to sleep near to, or spend much time in close proximity to, animals, which dramatically reduced any risk of catching disease from them.

The poor, and in particular the urban poor, lived very different lives and enjoyed few of these luxuries. They frequently lived in overcrowded cities, in houses where human waste was dumped into a pit close to the house. The very poor without houses could not depend on dry quarters, while in winter warmth was a luxury many of the poor had to do without. They ate badly, rarely enjoying meat, and suffered frequently from food shortages. The realities of life in such environments helps to explain the high mortality rates among the poorer classes in society. Illness and diseases like plague thrived amid their cramped homes, while famine and a poor diet made them easy prey for disease.

For the poor, the Black Death was by no means the first major outbreak of disease, although it was exceptional in its scale. Each time famine broke out it was accompanied by related illnesses, which devastated an already weakened population. In 1315, as the worst medieval famine gripped Ireland, the Annals of Loch Cé reported 'numerous wonderful diseases throughout all Erinn'[145]. This may have been the dysentery reported by John of Trokelowe in England at the time.[146] Even after the famine, the weakened survivors were vulnerable, and there were outbreaks of smallpox in the 1320s.

Aside from such outbreaks, day-to-day living also took its toll on the bodies of the poor. Eating rough bread ground their teeth down, exposing the pulp and leading to infection. In a world without antibiotics, this would certainly cause severe pain and could lead to sepsis, which was potentially fatal. There is also evidence of a population suffering from degenerative joint diseases from repetitive work, which would have made movement very painful.[147]

Although the medieval world was unable to deal with, or even comprehend, most of the diseases that caused the majority of fatalities in the medieval era, the medical profession still had a role. While the rich and powerful had personal physicians, there was a huge need for more easily accessible medics. On a daily basis in the towns of medieval Ireland people suffered wounds from violence that needed attention. In Cork, for example, in 1311 a man called John Berderne was struck with an axe on the head, yet he still survived.[148] It was people such as Berderne who would have needed the assistance of physicians and surgeons who were prepared to work with the poor. Some of these 'ordinary' physicians and surgeons survive in the historical records. One man, Maurice O'Hynnenan, a surgeon, was mentioned in 1317 on a list of people pardoned for crimes during the Bruce invasion, while another physician Gilcomde Doyrin was charged in 1311 with 'diverse trespasses and felonies'[149]. While there is no mention of social class, the fact such men were reduced to criminality indicates that they were unlikely to have been wealthy people.

Important as they were, such physicians and surgeons did not perform the most important medical role in the medieval world. This honour fell unquestionably to the midwife. Birth was the most dangerous single event most women experienced. Complications and bleeding could result in death, and the experience of midwives in this was crucial. Infection was a constant threat, and one not properly understood given the medieval analysis of how disease passed from person to person. The experience of midwives was crucial. While they would have understood the importance of cleanliness, they would not have necessarily been aware of its implications.

Midwives also dealt with issues around birth control and reproductive choices. Although there is only a limited amount of historical evidence on the subject, it appears that birth control was far less controversial than it is today. Contraception and abortion may have been very important to women who could not afford to have large families. Indeed, many clerics were writers on contraception and early-term abortifacients, including Peter of Spain and future Pope John XXI, who was described as a 'prolific writer on birth control techniques' by one historian.[150]

Medicine in the medieval world is a difficult subject to pin down. While it was hopelessly inadequate in so many ways, it nonetheless had a function. Whether this was to look after lepers condemned to a life of exclusion, or to attempt to heal some more complicated injuries such as cranial fractures, doctors, surgeons and in particular midwives were crucial to medieval life.

# 10

# Piracy, Looters and Storms: Travelling to 'Parts beyond the Seas'

In the early fourteenth century, Betto le Lumbard died far from his Italian homeland of Lombardy when he was killed by his servant in Clonmel, a small town on the Suir River in Tipperary. In the aftermath, the town authorities sealed Betto's house and, in particular, the strong chests he used to store his wealth. Despite these measures, in the following days Francis Malyzard, and several others acting for the Riccardi of Lucca, a famous Italian banking house, raided Betto's home. They forced open the chests and escaped with money and jewels worth 200 marks. Malyzard, presumably recovering a debt owed to the Riccardi, did not wait to be arrested but fled, probably making his way to his employers[151]. While this story gives us a far more cosmopolitan view of Anglo-Norman Ireland than we might expect, it also underscores just how important sea travel was to daily life. This interaction between a bank from Lucca and an Italian from Lombardy in a small town in medieval Ireland could not have happened without widespread and frequent sea travel.

The very functioning of government in Anglo-Norman Ireland was heavily dependent on naval travel. Ireland was ruled by English kings after the Norman invasion of 1169, which ensured there was a constant stream of officials and nobles back and forth across the Irish Sea to the royal court. While this naval travel was crucial for these international connections, it was also integral to transport and communications in Ireland. The rivers of the Shannon, Suir, Barrow, Nore, Liffey and Boyne were bustling with naval traffic, while all major towns were built on rivers. These medieval motorways saw crafts of all shapes and sizes ply their trade. Indeed, in the early fourteenth century the River Shannon was even patrolled by a war galley, powered by at least thirty-two oars, which the king had ordered to be built in 1305.

## Sea Travel

Despite the fact that everyday life in medieval Ireland was utterly dependent on waterborne transportation, it was, nevertheless, a hair-raising experience at the best of times. Medieval seafarers took to the water in ships that were little bigger than small sailing boats today. While there were numerous types of vessels, the most common ship used in the late medieval period was the cog. Compared to modern shipping, the cog was absolutely tiny. Measuring around twenty-five to thirty metres in length, it was scarcely bigger than two buses. While it supported platforms at either end, which provided limited shelter, it was by no means comfortable. The limited space on board was often shared by the crew, several passengers, animals and cargo. The most important function of the platforms at either end was defence. In the event of piracy they gave the ship's crew the advantage of added height and the ability to rain down arrows on the deck of an attacking vessel, which was, as we shall see, crucial[152].

Cogs were powered by one square sail, supported by a mast in the middle of the ship. This made them totally reliant on the wind. If winds died down, these ships could easily be stranded at sea, but for medieval mariners traversing the seas around Ireland, a lack of wind was rarely an issue. Indeed if anything, the opposite was frequently the case, as storms were one of the greatest hazards faced by sailors.

In the absence of accurate weather forecasts, mariners took their lives in their hands on any long-distance journeys where they had to travel far from the sight of land. Unless they were close to shore, they had no option but to endure unforeseen storms, which could easily result in death.

Many preferred long waits, or not to travel at all, to risking a stormy sea. In October 1171, when King Henry II crossed to Ireland with a fleet of 400 ships, he had to wait for sixteen days at Milford Haven for the weather to clear. Over forty years later, when John de Courcy, the first Earl of Ulster, attempted to sail to Ireland from Chester in 1204, he had to postpone travelling on fifteen consecutive occasions as he 'was evermore in danger and the wind always against him'.[153]

## Storms

If storms blew up, these tiny ships could be blown far off course. In 1346, John de Vere, the Earl of Oxford, was returning from Brittany, where Edward III was fighting the opening encounters of the One Hundred Years War. As his ship crossed the Celtic Sea between France and Ireland, a storm blew up, and he was blown so far off course that he eventually landed on the coast of Connacht. As the crew came ashore half naked, the Gaelic Irish plundered the ship and attacked the crew, and the earl was lucky to survive[154]. Similarly in 1313 two merchants, William Comptoun and Wolfram de Bristoll, were blown far off course to an island off the coast of Scotland. At the time, Scotland was at war with England and, unsurprisingly, the merchants were attacked, had all their goods stolen and again scarcely escaped with their lives.[155]

These, however, were among the luckier ones; the fate of those caught in a storm could be far worse. In one of the worst shipping disasters in medieval Irish history, the Treasurer of Ireland, Walter de Thornbury, along with around 150 others, were drowned at sea in 1313[156]. This incident provoked St Mary's Abbey, Dublin to make official copies of its charters when the abbot was about to travel 'to parts beyond the seas' that same year. They cited the 'dangers of the ways, and the peril of the seas'[157] as the reason.

## Looters

For merchants and sailors alike, coastal populations in Ireland could be a greater threat than any storm that damaged their ships. Such communities had little sympathy for shipwrecked sailors, often seeing them as potential sources of loot rather than victims. In 1306, a ship *The Nicholas of Doun* was wrecked by a 'severe tempest of the sea'[158] off the coast of Dublin. Many of the sailors died in the storm, but the surviving crew managed to come ashore at Portmarnock, north of the city. On this occasion they no doubt counted their blessings, as much of the ship's cargo of wines, spices, jewels, copper pots and wax were washed up close to the shore. Afterwards the crew and the some local people were able to rescue the goods and haul them onto the beach.

Soon the sailors found that the local people's aid were not as altruistic as it initially seemed. They viewed the sailors' misfortune as their opportunity. Within a short time they were getting drunk on the wine and began stealing the merchandise that had been rescued from the water. Later, over thirty men and women from the surrounding region ended up in court for stealing goods that had been rescued from the wreck[159]. This threat from overzealous scavengers paled into insignificance against the misfortune of encountering pirates.

## Pirates

Pirates roved the seas around Ireland, often not only raiding ships, but stealing entire vessels, before sailing to another port and selling the contents. In 1305, a ship owned by merchants in Dinon, Brittany, was stolen off the coast of northern France. The pirates sailed away with the cargo of sixty-six casks of wine. A few weeks later they turned up in the Irish port of Dundalk, where the pirates-turned-merchants sold the wine before eventually trying to sell the ship itself.

These actions, unsurprisingly, aroused the suspicions of the local authorities, who eventually seized one of the pirates: John Torald. Eventually the Breton merchants succeeded in having the vessel returned to them in a court case some time later.[160] Torald's activities highlighted how far medieval pirates were willing to travel to get their prize. In 1320, in a similar story, nine men from ports across the south of Ireland were accused of stealing a ship in Bordeaux, and killing the crew, nearly a thousand miles from home.[161]

Piracy also took place much closer to the shores of Ireland. In 1318 a ship called *le Mariota* was attacked by pirates in Dublin Bay, near Howth. They boarded the ship and stole its cargo, worth over £300. Not wanting to leave the vessel intact, they broke it up and sank it.[162]

While piracy was a major threat, when war erupted, merchants could face the prospect of being hounded by enemy fleets. The later thirteenth century war that broke out between the English and the Scots saw the sea lanes around Ireland increasingly militarised. In 1307, Hugh Biset, the Lord of Rathlin Island and the Glens of Antrim, was instructed to bring a galley of forty oars and other smaller galleys and vessels to attack the king's enemies around the islands of the west coast of Scotland. These fleets could have a devastating impact on travellers, as was seen a few years later when the Scots retaliated and pushed down into the Irish Sea.

Led by a man called Thomas Dun, the Scots increasingly made their presence felt off the Irish coast from 1311 onwards. After conquering the strategically important Isle of Man in 1313, they became a threat to shipping between England and Ireland. By 1315, the dangers posed by Thomas Dun and his fleet were illustrated when he raided the port of Anglesey in Wales, where much of the traffic between Dublin and Britain landed. The Scots even managed to make off with a ship, the *James of Caernarfon*.

In the following weeks the situation deteriorated so much that travel across the Irish Sea almost ceased. When a royal emissary John de Hothum travelled to Ireland in September, his passage was delayed for fear of Dun. De Hothum arrived in Chester on 20 September, but did not depart for Ireland until November, when he had secured a complement of eight ships and eighty-six men to protect him should he encounter Thomas Dun en route[163]. This threat was only eliminated when Dun was killed in 1317.

While the threats posed by the likes of Dun were rare, sea travel was a constant risk, whether from piracy or the weather. Nevertheless it was crucial to life as it existed in the Norman colony in Ireland, and indeed it would remain both as important and as dangerous for centuries to come.

**Lea Castle, Co. Laois**
(Eamonn Costello, 2013)

Lea Castle was one of the key Fitzgerald strongholds in the Midlands. It was here that Richard de Burgh, the Earl of Ulster and Lord of Connacht, was imprisoned in 1294–5 when he was kidnapped by John Fitzthomas. This sparked one of the many conflicts between the de Burghs and Fitzgeralds.

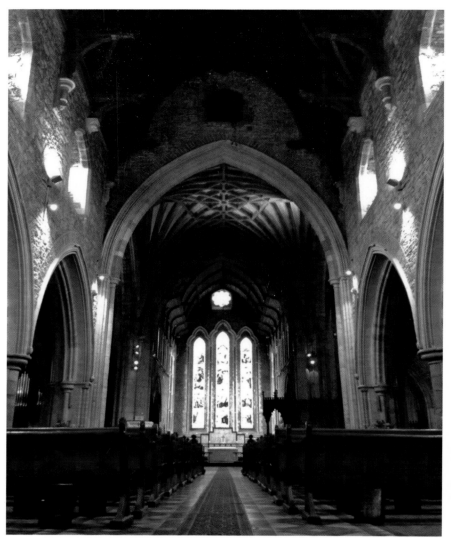

**St Canice's Cathedral, Kilkenny**

This magnificent structure was the seat of the Bishop of Ossory.

**The tomb of Bishop Richard Ledrede, St Canice's Cathedral, Kilkenny**

As Bishop of Ossory (1317–1361), Ledrede was one of the most controversial figures in fourteenth-century Ireland. After burning Petronilla di Midia for heresy in 1324, he spent much of the following two decades in exile after becoming embroiled in political intrigues. He returned to Ireland in 1347. He was in his nineties when he died in 1361.

**Glendalough, Co. Wicklow**
(Cormac Scully, 2013)

This remote, breathtaking valley situated in the Wicklow Mountains was the centre of the Diocese of Glendalough. In 1216 it was merged with the Diocese of Dublin. The fortunes of Glendalough waned in the following decades as the Archbishops of Dublin focused their energies on Castlekevin, a settlement a few miles to the north-east. These mountains were riven with warfare and revolt in the decades after 1270.

**Dublin Castle**
(Cormac Scully, 2013)

Most of the original early thirteenth-century structure is now gone, save the Records Tower. The castle was frequently used as a prison. In 1312, Fyngole McTorkoill devised a daring plan to free several prisoners. It failed, she was imprisoned, and the others involved were executed (see chapter 6).

**Kilkenny Castle**
(Eamonn Costello, 2013)

Built in the early thirteenth century, this impressive fortress was the seat of the Seneschals of Kilkenny in the fourteenth century. In 1391 the castle became the seat of the Earls of Ormond.

**The Longman of Kilfane, Co. Kilkenny**

An effigy of a Norman knight from the early fourteenth century.

Next page:
**St Patrick's Cathedral, Dublin**
(Cormac Scully, 2013)

One of Dublin's two cathedrals, it was here that the trial of the Knights Templar was held in January 1310.

## 11

# Medieval Dublin:
# A Tale of Two Cities

In 1303 Richard de Burgh, the Earl of Ulster, fought for his King Edward I in his ongoing wars in Scotland. In return for his service, he had a debt of over £11,000 waived. This astronomical sum was more than the colonial exchequer in Ireland could hope to receive in two years! In terms of average wages it amounted to over one million days' pay for a male labourer, or two million days remuneration for a female labourer. Such obscene and mind-boggling inequality was deeply engrained in medieval society. Indeed, there is scarcely a single story or topic in this book that doesn't illustrate some aspect of the very different worlds the rich and poor inhabited.

In rural areas this difference was not only obvious in the way people lived their lives, but it was also carved into the landscape. While the poor inhabited hamlets and villages, the nobility built large castles or hall houses of stone and timber. Castles literally towered over the surrounding countryside as a symbol of their owner's power and prestige.

## One Wall; Two Cities

In cities, while this vast inequality remained, the rich and the poor lived in close proximity, their lives closely intertwined. While massive cathedrals and stone castles such as Kilkenny Castle or Dublin Castle loomed high above towns, there was little to physically separate the rich and poor in the streets and alleys below. This was particularly evident in Dublin.

Among the 11,000 people who lived along the banks of the River Liffey in fourteenth-century Dublin[164], the very rich and the very poor were all crammed into a relatively small space. Situated primarily along the south bank of the river, Dublin was not the busiest port in Ireland, an honour that fell to New Ross. Nevertheless it was the most populous and pre-eminent town in Anglo-Norman Ireland due to the presence of the colonial administration and authorities within its walls.

While life in the city was increasingly under threat from the Gaelic Irish in the mountains to the south of the city, it was still possible for merchants to make money. Although the exchequer building scarcely 100 metres from the city walls had to be emptied of valuables each night for fear of attack[165], by day the city's streets were a hive of activity. Alongside bustling trade with great potential for merchants lived the city's poor, often in grinding poverty.

While the rich and the poor walked the same streets and interacted with each other, they experienced the city they inhabited in very different ways. This tale of two medieval cities within the one wall is starkly evidenced by the stories of two early fourteenth century Dubliners: William Douce and Adam son of Philip. In 1317 and early 1318 these two men's worlds collided in a dramatic fashion.

# William Douce

William Douce was born sometime in the late thirteenth century. Dublin is unlikely to have been his birthplace as there is no mention of his family residing in the city before the arrival of William. He first appears in the city records in the early fourteenth century. As with most medieval people, almost nothing is known about his early life, but by the opening years of the fourteenth century he was operating as a merchant in Dublin. It is possible that, like other wealthy merchants in the city, William was the scion of a rich merchant family in England who had emigrated to Dublin. This was the case for another successful medieval Dublin merchant, a contemporary of William's: Geoffrey Morton[166]. While Anglo-Norman Ireland was long past its heyday of the early 1290s, it was nonetheless somewhere men like William could advance.

First mentioned in a city court case in 1305[167], he reappeared several times in the following years, frequently seeking to have debts owed repaid to him. Later in 1305 in another court case, where John de Moreuill owed him twenty marks, William was for the first time referred to as a citizen of the city[168], a privilege that may have been bestowed on him in that year. This gave him important rights as a merchant, including the right to vote and the right to stand in mayoral and city office elections. His career continued to advance in 1306 when he was mentioned as working on behalf of the influential noble Piers de Bermingham, the Lord of Tethmoy, and ally of the powerful Fitzgerald family.[169]

Having accrued substantial resources, William Douce was also able to take advantage of the increasing mayhem that was sweeping across Ireland in the early fourteenth century when he rented lands from the king at Saggart.[170]

Situated in the shade of the Wicklow Mountains, Saggart was a dangerous area given that it had long been targeted in Gaelic Irish attacks. This usually had the effect of lowering rents as many were unwilling to take lands in such an area. William Douce, however, had sufficient resources to defend these lands. Indeed, even after the O'Tooles and O'Byrnes attacked the region in 1311, he requested to rent even more territory in the area. This was only possible as William was able to build a stone fortification[171], when many others were finding life in the region increasingly difficult.

After 1315, the economic life of Dublin was severely damaged when a crisis triggered by famine and the invasion of Edward Bruce enveloped Ireland. This was followed by an economic depression caused by cattle murrain, leaving the colony absolutely devastated by the mid-1320s. Despite these conditions, William Douce endured and became one of the key citizens of Dublin.

Despite successfully seeking an exemption from public office in 1316[172], which was granted by the king in 1327[173], he nevertheless went on to serve as mayor in the city for two years in the early 1320s and then again in the 1330s. As well as enjoying success in the municipal politics of the city, he was also a landowner of several pieces of property in Dublin and its suburbs.[174]

As a leader of medieval Dublin society, he also maintained strong connections with other merchant elites in other towns in Ireland. In 1324, when the powerful Kilkenny merchant and moneylender Alice Kyteler was accused of witchcraft, she fled from Kilkenny to Dublin. While in the city she spent time with Douce, and he was later cited by the Bishop of Ossory Richard Ledrede as aiding Kyteler (see chapter 13, p. 87).[175]

When he died, sometime before December 1343[176], his life in Dublin had been a success. Having arrived in the city in the late 1290s or early 1300s, he had become a successful city merchant, and on two occasions held the highest political office in the city. He had lived through some of the most violent chapters in the Dublin's history, but he had survived, not least because of his wealth.

## Adam son of Philip

While William was a success, many he passed in the city streets were not so fortunate. Indeed, they lived in a city far removed from the one of Douce's experience. While Douce planned his expanding agricultural interests in Saggart, the lives of the poor were often at best a struggle for survival. Lacking property or influence, their names, let alone details of their lives, were rarely regarded as being worth recording. We do get the glimpse of one such person when his life briefly crossed that of William Douce in late 1317. This man is known to us only as 'Adam son of Philip'. From what little we know of Adam he seems to have been a pauper, as in 1318 the only historical reference to his wealth stated that he had 'no chattels and no free land'[177].

For people such as Adam, life in Dublin in the early fourteenth century was extremely difficult; they frequently lived close to death. By the time the Bruce invasion was launched in 1315, Dublin had experienced numerous crises, which we have encountered in this book. Large sections of the city had been burned in 1301 and 1304, while the population had been ravaged by a famine in 1310. In 1315 Adam faced into yet another famine, in which he would suffer no matter what transpired.

As in the previous famine of 1310 (see chapter 4, p. 37), crime of all sorts skyrocketed during this period as people struggled to eat. By 1317 the price of wheat had reached twenty-four shillings per crannock, while oats had soared to sixteen shillings per crannock[178], some of the highest prices ever recorded in Ireland. It was people like Adam son of Philip who died from starvation when prices reached these levels. This was the context to Adam's sole record in history, without which we would never even know he existed.

In late 1317 or early 1318 Adam 'secretly entered a house on Winetavern Street in Dublin and stole a box which contained four marks'[179], which was a very substantial sum of money. The house he burgled belonged to none other than William Douce. Unfortunately for Adam son of Philip, he was caught and taken before a court. At his trial he did not face what might be termed an impartial jury, nor was it a collection of his peers. The jury included several members of the Taverner family and Nicolas Comyn, who, like William Douce, were members of the powerful merchant elite in the city. Unsurprisingly, they had little compassion for the plight of the poor in such desperate times when robbery was common. In many ways city life at the height of a famine was a battle between the rich and poor. The poor struggled to survive by theft as the rich struggled to maintain their wealth. Facing a jury and legal establishment of people who were wealthy, Adam son of Philip, a man of no property, was convicted and sentenced to death by hanging for his robbery[180]. On an unknown date after 24 February 1318, Adam son of Philip was brought to one of the gallows outside of Dublin and hanged, becoming just another of the numerous poor unfortunate Dubliners hanged for such crimes. Adam's life could not have been more different than that of William Douce. While the court that condemned him to death noted that he had 'no chattels and no free land', William Douce on the other hand participated in civic and economic life in Dublin until his death over twenty-five years later.

The conflict between the rich and poor fought out in burglaries, courts and ultimately on the city gallows was borne out of the collision of the two medieval cities that coexisted within the walls of Dublin. One was a city of opportunity for men like Douce; the other an endless struggle for people like Adam.

# The Rise and Fall of the Knights Templar in Ireland

I n 1314, the last Grand Master of the Knights Templar, Jacques de Molay, was burned at the stake outside Paris under the orders of the King of France, Philip the Fair. His excruciating death brought a conclusion to seven years of trials, executions and inquisitions that resulted in the destruction of one of the most powerful institutions of medieval Europe: the Knights Templar. Formed to protect pilgrims in Palestine during the early Crusades, this order of warrior monks developed into a complex religious order with an army and a vast business empire.

In 1307, however, the Templars came under sustained, co-ordinated and at times violent attack across Europe. Within a few years this organisation, which has been compared to an early multinational corporation, was all but eradicated. The destruction of the Templars brought an end to the order that had been at the heart of medieval society for nearly two centuries. The source of many myths, the extirpation of the Templars had sinister and far-reaching consequences, particularly in Ireland.

The fall of the Knights Templar can be traced back to the early months of 1291, far from western Europe. In April that year a vast host under the Mamluk Sultan Kalil besieged the city of Acre on the eastern shore of the Mediterranean Sea. Acre, a heavily fortified port city, was the last toehold of the Crusader Kingdom of Jerusalem. The kingdom had been conquered by Christians in the aftermath of the First Crusade in 1097, but throughout the thirteenth century it had slowly disintegrated.

Through April and May the defenders of Acre mounted a desperate defence against the Sultan's army. It was ultimately futile, and by 18 May the walls were breached. While the city fell, the Knights Templar continued to resist. They held out for another ten days in a large fortress overlooking the city harbour. On 28 May 1291, these last defenders of Acre were finally defeated. The Templars' fanatical defence cost them their lives; they were massacred to a man in a stand that gained an almost mythical status afterwards. Suicidal chivalry aside, the reality was that the fall of Acre effectively brought the Crusades to an end. While there would be continued skirmishes for a few years, it would be six centuries before a western army would conquer and occupy Palestine again.

After this crushing defeat of the Crusader armies, the future of the Knights Templar was uncertain. They initially hoped to organise a new crusade from Europe, but these aspirations faded as years of inactivity and procrastination followed. While the founding aim of the order – to protect pilgrims – was no longer relevant, they were still a remarkably powerful institution. Although the history of the Templars has been obscured in recent years by conspiracy theories, they were in fact among the most powerful organisations in medieval Europe, playing a very important role in everyday life.

Aside from their presence in the Middle East, the Knights Templar had established one of the most impressive economic networks across the continent to support what had become expensive warfare in the Holy Land. This included numerous religious institutions, farms and banking houses, which stretched across medieval Christendom from Jerusalem to Dublin. After nearly two centuries they had become an integral part of economic and social life in European society, whether they were fighting wars in the Middle East or not. Even in Ireland, one of the most distant places from the Middle East, the Templars played an important part of medieval life since the earliest days of the Norman colony.

## The Rise of the Templars in Ireland

The Templars' presence in Ireland had begun as it would end, in the midst of scandal. Shortly after the Norman invasion of Ireland, King Henry II was embroiled in the shocking murder of Thomas Beckett, the Archbishop of Canterbury. In an act of atonement for his guilt, Henry made large endowments to the Church, including the grant of lands in Ireland 'to the brothers of the Temple to defend the Holy Land of Jerusalem'[181].

As the Norman colony in Ireland was established, many other powerful landowners followed in Henry's footsteps and granted the Knights Templar lands. Over time the Knights Templar came to possess some of the most strategically important and valuable lands in Norman Ireland. In the southeast, they controlled lands on either side of the Barrow River estuary, commanding an important position overlooking what was the most important waterway in Anglo-Norman Ireland. Templar preceptories and houses were also a common feature in major settlements in colonial Ireland. With members constantly on the move across Europe, and in some cases on military expeditions to Palestine, they needed numerous lodging houses to house them. Known as frank houses, the Knights Templar operated what were in effect hostels for members of the order who were engaged in such travel. The Templar properties in the port towns of Drogheda and Wexford[182] almost certainly filled this role.

This presence in ports and towns across Ireland and every kingdom in western Europe gave the Templars a distinct advantage in terms of international trade and in particular the lucrative wine trade between western France, England and Ireland, which they dominated.[183] While they accrued large amounts of property and were involved in trade, it was unquestionably their financial operations that were the most innovative, lucrative and ultimately the most controversial. It was their financial operations that would ultimately bring the order to ruin.

As we have seen throughout this book, travel in the medieval period was hazardous at the best of times, due to both natural and human perils (see chapter 10, p. 71). This made the transportation of physical wealth and valuables time-consuming, difficult and dangerous. Through the twelfth and thirteenth centuries, the origins of the modern banking system began to emerge from an increasing need to transfer wealth across the continent, not least to the conquered lands of the Middle East. In the absence of electronic communication, the Templars' geographical spread and wealth enabled them to take advantage of this need. In order to facilitate easier and safer movement of wealth, they allowed travellers to deposit sums of money in one Templar preceptory in return for a written receipt. The traveller could then produce this receipt along the route at another preceptory in return for money, thus avoiding the difficulties involved in transportation of valuables. Through these activities the Templars became one of the earliest medieval transcontinental banks.

As they grew in wealth and were increasingly involved in other financial services, the Templars also began to lend money to the aristocracy and monarchs, who needed large sums to go on crusade. Such activities inevitably led to problems for the Templars. Kings, for example, tended to repay loans by farming out the right to collect taxes to the lender. In Ireland and other regions this saw the Templars become tax collectors of sorts. In Waterford, customs collected at the port and the city's fee farm (a rent owed to the Crown) was given to the Templars rather than the exchequer to repay debts.[184] Having combined two of the most unpopular professions, tax collecting and moneylending, the Templars' activities unsurprisingly drew increasing criticism and resentment.

## Problems Arise

After the fall of Acre, with resentment increasing at home and the order fulfilling no specific purpose in terms of its crusading mission, it was increasingly vulnerable to criticism. Simultaneously, they also had some very powerful debtors, including Philip the Fair, King of France, who sought to renege on the debts they owed. To compound these issues further, Philip the Fair increasingly had power and influence over the one man who both protected and had the potential to destroy the Templars: Pope Clement V.

In 1307, when rumours circulating about bizarre practices within the order reached Philip, he prepared to attack the weakened order and escape the debts he owed. Philip also eyed up the large possessions of the Templars in his Kingdom with avarice.

The rumours about the Templars included claims that they were in effect a heretical organisation who denied

God and practiced bizarre secret rituals. In early fourteenth century France, such accusations of heresy were explosive. Ideas around heresy in general had changed in France during the previous century. Any deviation from Christian teaching was increasingly interpreted as an act of Satan that needed to be violently suppressed.[185]

In this climate, an allegation of heresy and apostasy gave Philip the pretext he desired to violently attack the Templars, using the charge of heresy. Philip the Fair's assault on the Templars began on Friday, 13 October 1307[186]. In a surprise attack, nearly all Templars in France were arrested. Under torture, ludicrous confessions of heresy and idolatry were obtained. Armed with these confessions, Philip then attacked the wider Templar organisation outside his own kingdom; this process would soon arrive in Ireland. In order to do this he exercised his influence over Clement V, who in turn condemned the order. By November, what had been a major force in European society was under attack across the continent under these very serious charges. Orders were issued to arrest the Templars everywhere, including Ireland.

In England, the Templars were arrested on 9–11 January 1308. Due to the distances involved, the suppression of the Knights Templar in Ireland did not take place until 8 February. Across the colony, members of the order were arrested, although the fact that no ships were seized indicates that some Templars may have already fled the country. Their property was seized by royal officials, and those arrested were imprisoned in Dublin Castle.

## The Trial of the Templars in Dublin

Charges that had been based on rumour and confessions under torture in France made little sense in Ireland. Regardless of the veracity of the charges, orders were orders, and a trial began in St Patrick's Cathedral in January 1310. This was the first occasion where heresy trials of this kind had been conducted in Ireland. Three Dominicans and two Franciscans oversaw the trial. Aside from the charges against them, the Templars had done little in their 190-year history to ingratiate themselves to other orders. Their wealth and the favouritism shown to them by successive popes since their inception had caused envy from other orders.

The trial lasted for nearly six months, concluding in June. Unlike the trials in France, there is no evidence that torture was used. The verdict is not recorded, and may well have been postponed pending consultation with papal authorities.[187] The Templars themselves were returned to prison in Dublin Castle. While ambiguity surrounded the result of the trial in Dublin, it was clear the order's days were numbered due to what was happening elsewhere. In France in 1310, dozens of Templars had been burned at the stake for heresy under the order of Philip the Fair, who had ever-increasing control over the Pope (now resident in Avignon, a city in Philip's kingdom). Amid mounting pressure from Philip, Clement dissolved the order in 1312 and transferred its vast possessions to the Knights Hospitaller. This annihilation of the Templars was unparalleled in Irish or European history until the Reformation. Political action in the medieval period was rarely so decisive and/ or co-ordinated across the European continent. It was a terrifying illustration of the power of heresy charges.

In Ireland, the immediate consequences of the suppression of the order were far less severe than in France. The Templars were eventually released from captivity and were given a stipend of two pence a day on which to live. While this was generous by the standards of contemporary labourers, it represented a major decline in living standards for former Templars.

Unsurprisingly, the division of the Templars' lands created great tensions in Ireland. Noble families who had previously given lands to the Templars now sought to reclaim them rather than see them pass to the already powerful Order of the Knights Hospitaller as the Pope had decreed. This led to decades of disputes; as late as 1327 there were complaints that the Knights Hospitallers were illegally claiming lands that had once belonged to the Templars.[188] There were far more insidious consequences as well. The Templar trial imported the extreme views of heresy that had developed in France during the previous century, and within a few months the dangers posed by these ideas became apparent.

Religious life in Dublin had long been dominated by tensions between the two cathedrals in the city. While most cities had only one cathedral, Dubin had two: St Patrick's Cathedral and Christchurch Cathedral. They had constantly fought over which cathedral chapter had the right to elect the Archbishop of Dublin (technically, both did). In what appears to have been a continuation of this rivalry, in 1310 one of the inquisitors at the Templar trial, Thomas de Cheddesworth (a dean of St Patrick's) accused Philip de Braybrook (a canon of Christchurch) of being a relapsed heretic.

The charges were extremely weak, and appear to have been rooted in the tensions between the cathedrals rather than de Braybrook's beliefs. Nonetheless de Cheddesworth succeeded in having his opponent discredited and punished. De Braybrook was convicted of being a relapsed heretic, although he escaped the death penalty, which was the usual sentence for such a crime. Instead he was committed to the priory of All Hallows, where he was condemned to stay for a year on a diet of bread, beer and one meal each day save Fridays and Wednesdays, when he had to fast.

As 1310 drew to a close, it was clear that this new (and later to prove deadly) interpretation of heresy had taken root in Ireland. While the demise of the Templars shocked fourteenth-century Ireland, worse was to come. As we shall see in the story of Alice Kyteler, within fourteen years these ideas brought witch burnings to Ireland.

# 13

# Ireland's First Witch?

Although it was by no means the biggest market town in Ireland, medieval Kilkenny was still a prosperous settlement. Situated on the upper reaches of the Nore River, the town overlooked a rich hinterland. In the decades after the Norman invasion, Kilkenny thrived. To the medieval traveller the settlement was clearly wealthy – there were numerous stone buildings such as priories, hospitals, and after 1250 an expensive but increasingly necessary defensive town wall. By the mid thirteenth century the town had grown to occupy a long stretch of land abutted by two enormous buildings. To the south lay the seat of the local lords, the great fortress of Kilkenny Castle, while to the north stood the towering edifice of St Canice's Cathedral, the seat of the Bishop of Ossory.

The town's success was due in part to the arrival of merchants from across Europe throughout the thirteenth century. While the overland route was increasingly prone to outlaws and thieves, they could easily ship their goods up and down the Nore River to the nearby port of New Ross. Among such families to trade in Kilkenny was the Flemish merchant family, the Kytelers. In 1277 William Kyteler of Ypres received permission from the king to ship 'his goods and merchandise by the sea coast of England and Ireland into Ireland'[189].

Like many others, William chose to settle in Kilkenny, and in 1280 Jose (perhaps his son) died and was buried in the town.[190] In the coming years the Kytelers became wealthy merchants and moneylenders while other extended family members would become mayors and sheriffs of the town. It was neither their mercantile nor civic activities, however, that would give the Kytelers immortality in medieval Irish history. In the 1320s they became embroiled in a dispute with a local bishop, which had far-reaching consequences, not only for the Kyteler family, but ultimately for thousands across Ireland and indeed Europe. After the dispute several people would be dead and one of the Kytelers would have disappeared, while the name of the Bishop of Ossory, Richard Ledrede, would be synonymous with medieval barbarism. It also marked the beginning of the earliest phase of European witch-hunts that would continue for centuries.

## Alice Kyteler

The Kytelers established themselves as a powerful family in the region. When Alice (most likely William Kyteler's daughter) married in the early 1280s, the family's wealth allowed her to wed the powerful William Outlaw. The Outlaw family were not only rich merchants and moneylenders, but also political leaders of the Norman colony in Ireland. Roger Outlaw held the positions of Deputy Justiciar and Chancellor, and was also the Prior of the Knights Hospitaller in Ireland. Unsurprisingly the couple's son, also called William, was able to rise to the position of Mayor of Kilkenny by 1305.

In the early fourteenth century William senior died, and Alice sought a new husband. This was by no means unusual;

in an era of high mortality rates and low life expectancy second and even third marriages were not uncommon. By 1303 Alice was married again, on this occasion to Adam le Blund, another wealthy merchant from the nearby town of Callan. The wealth that Adam and Alice amassed was astounding. Around the same time there is a reference to a sum of £3,000 owned by the couple. They also loaned £500 to the Crown for the ongoing wars in Scotland. Given their position as moneylenders it is unsurprising that the couple had enemies. They were falsely accused and ultimately acquitted of murder at around this time.[191]

Alice appears to have had no further children after William, and devoted her energy and influence into aggrandising her only son. In April 1306 Adam le Blund (her second husband) signed over all his property and wealth to his stepson William.[192] Shortly afterwards le Blund died, and by 1309 Alice had married her third husband Richard de Valle. Like her previous husbands, de Valle was wealthy, owning substantial tracts of land in neighbouring Tipperary. Little is known about their relationship, but de Valle too was dead by 1316. After the death of Richard de Valle, Alice had to sue her deceased husband's heir to get a third share of his property, as was a widow's right. While it appeared that she had done nothing illegal, it was clear that Alice and her son William were financially benefiting from the early and frequent deaths of her spouses.

Despite the premature death of Alice's third husband, she was still among the most eligible women in Kilkenny, given that the key prerequisite for medieval marriage contracts was the financial position of the prospective partner. For her fourth marriage Alice Kyteler wedded John le Poer, a member of an aristocratic family. While Kyteler was heading towards her fourth marriage, another immigrant was arriving in Kilkenny, a man whose presence would transform the life of Alice Kyteler, and many others in the town.

## Bishop Richard Ledrede

In autumn 1317, Richard Ledrede, a Franciscan who had been appointed Bishop of Ossory, took up his seat in St Canice's Cathedral in Kilkenny. Ledrede, originally from England, had come to Ireland from Avignon where the papal court had relocated in 1309. Arriving in the region, Ledrede found the countryside utterly devastated by war. In early 1317 the armies of Robert and Edward Bruce had rampaged through the area and, while avoiding fortified Kilkenny, had swept through the south of the county.

Ledrede was unperturbed by this chaotic environment, having been imbued with fundamentalist ideas of Christianity in an Avignon reeling from the brutal trials of the Knights Templar. Arriving in Kilkenny directly from Avignon, he described himself as 'nourished, educated and promoted' by papal politics.[193] These politics included the violent annihilation of the Knights Templar. He appears to have been profoundly affected by these events and infused with the ideas of heresy that dominated the trials (see chapter 12, p.81). He fervently believed that such heresies and Satanism were not only at large in the world, but that these threats needed to be violently rooted out.

While Ledrede had developed these ideas in Avignon, they were not completely new in Anglo-Norman Ireland. They had already shaped the trial of the Knights Templar and then Phillip de Braybrook in 1310 (see chapter 12, p.81). Thus, in Kilkenny, Ledrede found a society not just brutalised by war but also one aware of his extremely austere and intolerant version of Christianity. This potent mix created a very dangerous foundation on which a man like Ledrede could indulge his anti-heretical fantasies.

If anyone was uncertain of his view of the world, shortly after his arrival in October 1317 he warned that if 'anyone in the diocese is aware that any person is preaching heresy therein, he is to give information thereof within a month after it has come to his knowledge'[194]. No one could have envisaged how much Ledrede would develop the idea, but by the 1320s he would terrorise the town with heresy trials.

While Ledrede was railing against heretics, Alice Kyteler married her fourth, and as far as is known, her final husband, John le Poer. John had much in common with Alice Kyteler's other husbands. He was powerful and wealthy, and, unfortunately, within a few years of marriage he was also on his deathbed. In 1324 he was described as 'emaciated, his nails were torn out and all hair removed'[195]. After a fourth relationship, which was relatively short yet very advantageous for Alice, her former stepchildren began to get suspicious. Her propensity to enrich herself and her son in these relationships had led to the disenfranchisement of the stepchildren, and now they wanted justice.

## Accusations of Witchcraft

Alice Kyteler soon found herself to be the subject of accusations that she was killing her husbands for her own financial benefit. The symptoms displayed by le Poer have been recognised in recent decades as being compatible with arsenic poisoning.[196] In 1324, in the absence of toxicology reports, there was little evidence to convict Alice Kyteler. In such instances, however, she was open to the charge of *maleficium* – the use of sorcery to harm others.

Accusations around the use of folk magic and potions to harm others had a long history in what was a deeply superstitious society.[197] However, in this new world of rapidly changing religious beliefs, people like the Bishop of Ossory did not believe in such traditions rooted in paganism. Ledrede instead interpreted the accusations as heresy – that Alice Kyteler had acted in league with demons. Heresy as a crime, as the brutal trials of the Templars had illustrated, was a far more serious charge.

On hearing of the accusations and rumours about Alice Kyteler, this confirmed Ledrede's belief that he was surrounded by heretics. He later stated there were 'many heretical sorceresses who practised all kinds of sorcery'[198] in Kilkenny. In response to this perceived threat he set in motion a series of events that would not only bring the Church into conflict with the secular authorities, but shock medieval Ireland to the core.

Having been on the lookout for heresy since arriving in Kilkenny, he quickly established his own inquisition to investigate what he considered to be heresy charges. Heavily influenced by the Templar trial in France over a decade earlier, he now conjured up similarly ludicrous charges against Alice Kyteler and several others, including her son.

While Alice Kyteler's stepchildren may well have had legitimate grievances, Ledrede transformed the case. He accused her of making sacrifices to demons while also having sexual relations with a demon known as Robin Artisson, who took the form of a black dog or a black man. He went on to accuse her of using the skull of a decapitated robber as a cauldron for the boiling of her sacrificial offerings. These were clearly influenced by and reminiscent of the charges levelled against the Knights Templar over a decade previously.

Ledrede also expanded the charges beyond Alice Kyteler and her son William Outlaw, creating a widespread conspiracy. Along with four men he also charged three women from the Galryssn family, as well as Petronilla of Meath, her daughter Sara, Alice Carpenter and Annota Lange.[199] What connection they had to the case is not clear.

Despite such dangerous charges, Alice Kyteler and her son were formidable opponents for the bishop. Through their financial and political connections they could rely on some of the most powerful people in Ireland to hinder Ledrede's case against them. Among her allies were Arnold le Poer and Roger Outlaw, the Chancellor of Ireland. Arnold le Poer, who did most to obstruct Ledrede, was the Seneschal of Kilkenny, and was probably related to Alice's last husband John.

## Arnold le Poer, Seneschal of Kilkenny

Le Poer had strong motivations for resenting the charges, aside from the fact that Alice and her son were his relatives. As Seneschal of Kilkenny, one of the greatest threats to his power was the Church. Ledrede as bishop ruled over his own ecclesiastical jurisdiction within the territory under le Poer's control. Given the tenacious opposition le Poer mounted against Ledrede, he appeared to interpret the bishop's actions as an infringement on his authority. Le Poer was willing to use whatever means necessary to dispose of potential rivals. In 1310 he had killed John de Boneville when the two had vied for the position of Seneschal of Carlow.[200]

Richard Ledrede proved to be both fearless and relentless. Initially he was constantly evaded by the Kytelers. When he pressed charges in Kilkenny, Alice fled the city to Dublin, but her son William Outlaw remained behind. As Outlaw was supported by Arnold le Poer, Ledrede found it almost impossible to prosecute him.

Initially slow to use violence against a man of the cloth, le Poer pleaded with the bishop to withdraw the charges. After failing on this score he resorted to the tactics he understood best: he simply arrested the bishop and imprisoned him so that Ledrede could not hear the case. This was both a significant underestimation of Ledrede and a serious error on le Poer's part. The bishop saw heretics in everyone who opposed him, and refused to back down. Instead he placed Kilkenny under interdiction, which in effect suspended religion in the city. This served to rally the population to his side.

Ledrede orchestrated widespread opposition to le Poer's action, and then masterfully co-ordinated his release from prison in a manner that would impress any modern spin doctor. When he was released he refused to leave his cell in Kilkenny Castle until a great procession to the cathedral had been arranged.

Freed, and arguably more powerful than he had been before, he pressed ahead with the charges against Kyteler's son William. Ledrede's attempts were soon derailed, though, when he was summoned by the Dublin authorities to answer charges levelled by le Poer over his activities in Kilkenny. While no doubt aimed to delay the case against Outlaw even further, le Poer may have had more malign motives; Richard Ledrede refused to travel to Dublin, claiming he feared that Arnold le Poer would attack him along the road.

The situation continued to intensify when Alice Kyteler herself now accused Ledrede of making false accusations against her, and he was once more summoned to appear in Dublin. The bishop later claimed that le Poer again tried to have him killed along the road, but he made the trip nonetheless, taking a clandestine route through the mountains and arriving safely in the city.

Appearing in Dublin, the bishop began to gain the upper hand, eventually securing warrants against those he accused of witchcraft. Alice Kyteller now realised that she could no longer be protected by her political allies. Recognising the dangers, she fled the country and was never seen or heard of again. While at first it may have seemed that she was overly cautious, in time it would be proved that she alone had judged the issue correctly.

## Prosecutions

Having effectively neutralised the powerful political opposition he faced, Ledrede pushed ahead with several trials and had the accused in Kilkenny arrested. These included Alice Kyteler's son William Outlaw and another woman, Petronilla de Midia. While William Outlaw was found guilty, he was protected by numerous powerful allies. Petronilla, a servant, was not so fortunate. In June 1324 she was tortured, after which she admitted guilt in front of a large crowd. After this brutal punishment Ledrede had her burned at the stake.

The fanatical bishop was by no means finished. He went on to accuse others who had aided the Kytelers of heresy or protecting heretics. These included the powerful Roger Outlaw, Prior of the Knights Hospitaller, although Outlaw proved too powerful and was acquitted. Others were not so lucky. Arnold le Poer, who had done so much to stop the bishop, was charged with heresy in 1328. Although he did not live to see his trial, he was nonetheless humiliated. After le Poer died in Dublin Castle awaiting trial, he was refused a Christian burial as he had the outstanding charge of heresy against him. His body was left to rot unburied in Dominican Priory of St Saviour's for several months following his death in March 1329. William Outlaw did survive, although he had to agree to reroof the cathedral in Kilkenny with lead as a penance. This proved disastrous. In 1332 the bell tower collapsed (presumably under the weight of the lead), destroying much of the cathedral[201]; an incident that no doubt fuelled the belief that Alice Kyteler had been in league with demons.

The long-term impacts were far darker than a collapsed church or the grisly demise of Arnold le Poer. One contemporary of the events, Friar John Clyn of Kilkenny, a fellow Franciscan of Ledrede, wrote of the death of Petronilla di Midia 'it was not seen or heard of from times past that anyone in Ireland before her suffered the legal penalty of death for heresy'[202]. The Church was increasingly gaining control over all matters spiritual, and those outside their view of the world were seen and treated more and more as heretics, whether real or imagined. Unfortunately for several Gaelic Irish people, whose faith in some aspects of Christianity had been tested since the Norman invasion, this would prove disastrous (see chapter 14, p. 95).

The impact of Richard Ledrede's relentless hunt of Alice Kyteler and William Outlaw, and his ultimate execution of Petronilla di Midia, also marked the beginning of a darker trend in European history. This was among the earliest known cases where a woman was burned for heresy. It was also the first time that the accused was charged with having sexual relations with demons. Sadly, it was not the last. These accusations would become the hallmark of later witchcraft trials across Europe, which would see thousands executed in barbaric ways, just like Petronilla di Midia. It was the summer of 1324 in Anglo-Norman Ireland when this process of religious fundamentalism, shaped in France, began to move its tentacles into wider society. The results were disastrous.

# 14

# A Heretic in the 'Isle of Saints and Scholars'

On 11 April 1328, a few days after the Easter celebrations, Dublin witnessed one of the more gruesome events in its history. An unforgettable exposition of brutality took place in public, east of the city walls on Hoggen Green. Now called College Green, Hoggen Green was surrounded by some of medieval Dublin's major religious foundations. To its east stood the Priory of All Hallows, while the nunnery of St Mary de Hogges was situated to the south. The proximity of the city's faithful did not prevent the authorities in 1328 from proceeding with their cruelty. If anything, it was for their benefit.

Having just celebrated the resurrection of Jesus Christ a week previously, Dubliners were about to witness another man, Adam Dubh O'Toole, being executed for his unorthodox beliefs. O'Toole was burned at the stake.

While barbarism of this kind is often associated with the medieval period, acts with this degree of macabre cruelty were comparatively rare. Executions were common, but the preferred method was hanging; this was one of the earliest recorded public burnings in Dublin. It is unquestionable that the medieval mind had a penchant for public displays of brutality. Whilst this fondness could be indulged on occasion, events as vicious as a burning remained comparatively rare.

In 1311, the bakers of Dublin were tied to horses and hauled through the city streets after it was discovered that they were tampering with weights of flour in their bread. Five years later, in 1316, a thief called Roger de Fynglas was sentenced to death by hanging, but for an unknown reason he was instead returned to a cell in Dublin Castle and condemned 'there to stay without having food until he be dead'[203]. On occasion there had been even worse displays, which amounted to nothing short of gratuitous torture. These were most common in the deepening conflict between the Gaelic Irish and the Anglo-Normans. In 1277 Brian O'Briain was pulled apart between two horses by his erstwhile Norman allies when their relationship turned sour.

The fate that awaited the victim outside Dublin in 1328 was arguably worse still. His death would be excruciatingly slow, as flames would literally cook his flesh before he succumbed to burns. If he was lucky he would choke quickly from the smoke. While it was the earliest recorded burning in Dublin, it was not the first in Ireland. Only four years earlier, a woman, Petronilla de Midia, had been burned to death in Kilkenny (see chapter 13, p. 87). These were not just two coincidental cases of brutality; such an unusual and cruel punishment was generally reserved for heretics.

While Petronilla di Midia was almost certainly innocent of the charges, the man who mounted the pyre in 1328, Adam Dubh O'Toole, was probably guilty. He had rejected the cornerstones of Christianity and was horrifically punished for his beliefs. The story of his brutal end had its origins not only in Adam's own life but deep in his family's history over the previous 150 years since the Norman invasion of the 1160s.

Consumed by flames in Dublin during the spring of 1328, it was in the Wicklow Mountains that his story began. His heresy had been fomented amid deep-seated bitterness among the dispossessed Gaelic Irish, who had suffered greatly in the aftermath of the Norman colonisation of Ireland.

Long before Adam Dubh O'Toole was born, prior to the Norman invasion of Ireland, his extended family occupied rich farmlands in south Kildare, in the Gaelic Kingdom of Leinster. In the years immediately following the Norman Conquest, they struggled and failed to accommodate themselves in the emerging Norman colony in Ireland. Even though they paid homage to the King of England, Henry II, when he arrived in person in 1171, it was all to no avail. All the lands of medieval Leinster, including those of the O'Tooles, were taken by the Norman leader Richard de Clare. Known to history as Strongbow, de Clare had many followers who had fought for him and expected to be repaid with land. By the late 1170s the homelands of the O'Tooles had been given to Walter de Riddlesford, a Norman knight.

Adam Dubh's forefathers found themselves increasingly unwelcome in Anglo-Norman Ireland, and were forced east into the inhospitable Wicklow Mountains. There they settled on lands granted to them by a family member, Lorcan O'Toole, the Bishop of Glendalough.[204] In the mountain passes of the Glen of Imaal and Glenmalure, the O'Tooles eked out an existence in what was a harsh environment. For the same reasons that these idyllic glens attract tourists today, they were not conducive to human habitation in the twelfth century; they are remote, inhospitable, poor lands, which were particularly harsh in winter.

In the years after their transplantation, little is known of the activities of Adam Dubh's family. A silence in the historical record indicates that they were unable to mount any effective resistance to the Norman Conquest, or certainly no resistance that the Normans deemed worthy of record. There was one event, however, which bucked this trend.

In 1209, scores of citizens of Anglo-Norman Dublin were massacred as they celebrated a festival a few kilometres south of the city when they were attacked by the Gaelic Irish from the mountains in a surprise raid. Such was the devastation that more settlers had to be enticed from Bristol. This, however, was an isolated incident. While it is difficult to measure or find evidence of a sentiment in records, it appears that, following the conquest, a deep resentment and frustration set in among the Gaelic Irish. They were increasingly disenfranchised and alienated from the society taking hold around them. As the legal framework for Anglo-Norman Ireland was established, they found themselves living in a country with many of the characteristics of an apartheid society.

In this new world being forged by the Anglo-Normans, the Gaelic Irish were very much outsiders. Not only had the O'Tooles lost their lands, but the very basis of the religious ideas that they had held for centuries was undermined. For several centuries prior to the Norman invasion, the influence of Christianity had grown in Gaelic Ireland. Gaelic kings had rejected ideas that their power derived from nature, and instead turned to the Christian belief that they were divinely ordained to rule by God.

Following the invasion, however, Gaelic society suffered a detrimental blow when the Church supported the conquest. In 1155, Pope Adrian IV had officially supported a Norman invasion of Ireland, and articulated a very dim view of the Gaelic Irish. According to Geraldis Cambrensis, a Norman chronicler, Pope Adrian IV saw an invasion of Ireland as 'enlarging the boundaries of the Church, checking the descent into wickedness, correcting morals and implanting virtues'.[205] When the invasion occurred, the Church hierarchy in Ireland in turn supported the conquest that inflicted so much misery and acknowledged King Henry II as overlord.[206] It was increasingly difficult for the Gaelic Irish kings to use this God as a justification for their rule when representatives of that same God were sanctioning their destruction. In Wicklow, the situation for the O'Tooles was even worse, as they had to endure clerics directly participating in their subjugation.

In 1216, the lands they had settled in the mountains and the entire Diocese of Glendalough were merged with the Norman-controlled Diocese of Dublin. Living on Church lands, they now became tenants of the Norman archbishop Henry of London and his successors. While few tensions arose in the first decades, famine, poverty and hardship changed the situation drastically in the 1270s.

The early years of that decade witnessed ferocious weather and famine across Ireland, and in particular in the Wicklow Mountains. In these difficult conditions, decades of resentment finally gave way and the O'Tooles in desperation began to raid colonial settlements in search of food. Immediately these actions put them at odds with the archbishop, their feudal lord. The archbishop called in Justiciar James D'Audley, but was ultimately able to calm the situation through negotiations.

In the following years, a full-scale revolt broke out in the mountains. The O'Tooles were joined by the O'Byrnes, and eventually the traditional Gaelic kings of Leinster, the McMurroughs. The Church was by no means a bystander in the ensuing conflict. In 1274 a punitive raid into the mountains was led by none other than the Grand Master of the religious order of the Knights Hospitaller in Dublin. He led a large contingent of warrior monks from their foundation at Kilmainham. While ultimately he was defeated and captured in the mountains, actions like this undermined the influence of Christianity among the O'Tooles.

While very little is known about the specific religious ideas of the O'Tooles in the later thirteenth century, there were indications that Christianity was as not as dominant as once imagined in Gaelic Ireland. In 1256 a letter made its way to the Pope from the remote diocese of Raphoe in north-west Ireland with alarming news. The bishop, a Dominican called Mael Padraig O'Scannal, informed the Pope that some of his flock were worshipping idols.[207]

This period also witnessed the emergence of a myth that Gaelic Ireland would be saved by a messianic Gaelic hero, Aedh Eanghach, which was deeply worrying from a Christian point of view. In some versions of the myth, Aedh gained his powers not from the Christian God who had supported the conquest but from Mother Nature.[208] These incidents are not necessarily evidence that Gaelic Ireland was witnessing a widespread pagan revival, but rather that some were seeking new ways in which to understand the world around them. Christianity as they had once understood it was no longer fit for purpose.

These events were all happening against a backdrop of increased violence and warfare in Wicklow. The revolt that broke out in the 1270s ended eventually in the assassination of Art and Muirchertach McMurrough in Arklow in 1282. The fact this murder was organised by Justiciar, and also Bishop of Waterford, Stephen de Fulbourne, can have done little to improve Gaelic Irish respect for Church authorities.

The peace was not to last, and serious violence broke out again in 1295. Soon the Gaelic Irish began to enjoy notable victories against the colonists, making life in the mountains intolerable for them. It was this world into which Adam Dubh O'Toole was born; a Gaelic society frequently at war with the Norman authorities and with high levels of bitterness and distrust towards a Church hierarchy that had clearly rejected them.

In this world of medieval Wicklow, criticism of the Church and even its ideas can only have found fertile ground. Adam O'Toole's family were effectively at war with their Norman overlord, the Archbishop of Dublin, on and off after 1295. The archbishop's administrative centre at Castlekevin, once a thriving settlement, was reduced to ruins on several occasions. Frequently tenants had to flee the area in fear for their lives. It was clear that the Anglo-Norman authorities could not maintain their tokenistic control over the region indefinitely. By 1326, when a valuation of the archbishop's estates was carried out, Glendalough and Glenmalure were no longer mentioned, indicating that they had finally fallen from his control.

What this meant in terms of religious ideas is difficult to ascertain. When Adam Dubh was captured in 1328, it is clear that he had rejected the core tenets of Christianity. He was tried at an ecclesiastical court and found guilty on several charges. Adam reputedly denied the incarnation of Jesus Christ, rejected the concept of the Holy Trinity and called Mary a harlot. He also went on to deny the resurrection of the dead, while proclaiming that scripture was nothing more than fables. Finally, and perhaps most interestingly, he questioned the bona fides of the papacy. While the Pope of the day, John XXII, was more sympathetic to the plight of the Gaelic Irish than his predecessors[209], his deputations to King Edward II did not effect any change in circumstances for those living in the mountains of Wicklow.

The veracity of the charges, brought in a climate fuelled by the widespread conflict between the Gaelic Irish and the Normans, are impossible to prove from the distance of nearly seven centuries. There is strong evidence, however, that the charges against Adam had some basis. They were far more realistic than the ridiculous charges levelled against Alice Kyteler, which included the accusation that she had sexual relations with demons. The charges brought against Adam Dubh O'Toole were based on theological points, while his life experience lent itself to a hostile attitude to the Church authorities.

Unfortunately for Adam, his world, where Christian ideas made little sense, collided with one where the Christian Church was increasingly intolerant of views that in any way challenged its hegemony. Ireland in 1328 was still gripped by the aftermath of the Alice Kyteler trials; later that year Richard Ledrede, the Bishop of Ossory, accused the Prior of Kilmainham, Roger Outlaw, of protecting heretics. In this climate there were few who were in a position to argue for clemency for a heretic, particularly a Gaelic Irish heretic.

Suffering a similar fate to Petronilla di Midia, Adam Dubh O'Toole was burned alive outside Dublin shortly after Easter 1328. His death did not exterminate the heresy; like so many others throughout history, his persecutors killed the person but failed to kill the idea. In 1331 a letter to Pope Edward III referred to the heresy of Adam Dubh, saying that his ideas had spread even after his death.[210] In 1353 two more Gaelic Irish men were burned at Bunratty by the Bishop of Waterford, Roger Cradock, perhaps more evidence that such ideas continued to have currency in

Ireland. While these ideas never became mainstream in Gaelic society, the role of some Church authorities in the first two centuries after the Norman invasion questioned the beliefs of many Gaelic Irish people. When these ideas clashed with the increasing fundamentalism of the Christian Church after the Templar trials in the early fourteenth century, many were punished severely for such unorthodox beliefs.

# 15

# An Irishman in China

When the Archbishop of Dublin, John de Sanford, died on 2 October 1294, monks in Dublin were faced with a daunting challenge. Not only did two rival cathedrals in the city have to agree on a successor, who had to be elected, but they were also faced with what were almost impossible deadlines. They had to seek permission from the King Edward I to hold the election, which involved someone travelling to and from England. In accordance with Church rules, however, the election also had to be held within ninety days of the death of the previous bishop. Finally, the new archbishop then had to travel to the papal court in Rome within three months of his election[211] to receive the Pope's blessing. While these deadlines could be easily met today, in the thirteenth century they were nigh on impossible. In 1294, royal approval did not arrive in Dublin within the ninety days stipulated, and when the new Archbishop Thomas de Cheddesworth was elected, he also failed to make the journey to Rome in time[212]. While the delay was in part down to political wrangling, it was also as a result of the incredible difficulties posed by travel in the medieval world.

Even in the case of national emergencies, travel was still painstakingly slow. In July 1315, Edward II, King of England, heard rumours that the Scots had invaded the Anglo-Norman colony in Ireland. The incident about which he was inquisitive was the greatest political and military crisis medieval Ireland had ever faced – a huge Scots army had indeed landed on the Ulster coast. While Edward was still wondering about what was happening, the invasion was over a month old – it had begun on 26 May. On 10 July, Edward, trying to keep up with events – in a medieval sense of the word – wrote to several Norman lords in Ireland asking for an update on the Scots' invasion. These letters trotted their way across England, through the north of Wales to Holyhead and across the Irish Sea. Arriving in Dublin, they then began a dangerous and arduous journey through what was an ever more lawless Ireland to reach their recipients. Crisis or not, this request for urgent news did not travel fast. Assuming that the replies were drafted shortly after the letters were received, they took between two and four months to travel the 600 miles to Ireland. The earliest response was composed by Richard de Clare, the Lord of Thomond, on 8 September 1315,[213] while the last known response was written on 2 November by Thomas de Mandeville, the Seneschal of the Earl of Ulster.[214] This is not particularly surprising given the difficulties posed by travelling.

## The Royal Highway

The fastest overland transport was by horse on roads that were no more than dirt tracks. These were often impassable in poor weather. Indeed, the situation was so bad by the late thirteenth century that a 1297 Parliament noted, 'the royal highway is now, in many places so overgrown and blocked by the thickness of quickly growing wood that scarcely anyone, even on foot can pass through'[215]. When travellers weren't scrambling through bushes and forests, they faced the greatest threat in medieval Ireland: other people. Nobody was safe on remote roads. In 1310 a monk from Jerpoint Abbey was forcibly stopped on the highway between the towns of Wells and Kilory, where he was robbed of his horse and cloth to the value of forty shillings.[216] Even royal officials were not safe. In 1314 Alexander le Convers, the King's clerk, was robbed of 660 pounds destined for Ireland as he made his way through north Wales.[217] Murders and rapes were not uncommon either. In a world like this where travel, even in the case of emergencies, was incredibly slow, one might imagine that people simply lived intensely localised lives. From our modern viewpoint, travel in this world scarcely seems worth it. For medieval people, however, who did not know of paved roads, cars, electricity, the internet or even telegrams, spending much of their time walking or on horseback was just part of life. While the poor peasantry needed the permission of their lord's manor court to travel long distances, and rarely had the resources to board ships, those with greater freedom and resources did travel extensively. War took people from medieval Ireland to regions all over Europe, the farthest being the Crusades in the Middle East. Contingents from Ireland had participated in the Crusades; the Lord of Trim, and one-time Justiciar of Ireland, Geoffrey de Geneville, had been in the Middle East with King Edward I in the 1270s.

Traders also travelled long distances as part of everyday life. Having no alternative, many were often forced to repeat journeys several times transporting goods when it was not possible to use rivers. In 1282 a porter was hired to transport wheat and oats purchased at a fair in Ballysax in County

Kildare to Dublin.[218] Not only did he do the thirty-five mile journey overland, but he had to repeat the trek thirty-one times with a cart hauled by two horses, each mission taking several days! People also travelled great distances across the continent as well. The presence of exotic spices such as ginger and nutmeg in Dublin's markets was a testament to this. Due to such travel, society was far more multicultural in late medieval Ireland than we might imagine. In Anglo-Norman ports, the background noise was nothing short of a cacophony of voices and languages. Aside from the early forms of Irish and English we might expect, antecedents of modern French, Italian and Flemish filled docks and markets. Genoese merchants were active in Ireland in the late thirteenth century. Indeed, one of them, Hugh del Post rented land around St Mullins in Carlow in 1285.[219]

There were also more unusual guests from time to time. In 1353 the Hungarian soldier of fortune George Grissaphan, after having a crisis of conscience, became a hermit and travelled on pilgrimage to the holy site of Lough Derg.[220] Yet it wasn't just continental Europeans who made these long, arduous journeys across Europe bringing stories of distant lands; there were many from Ireland who embarked on incredible journeys as well. While many sailors and soldiers journeyed overseas through trade or war, some clerics travelled much longer distances. It was by no means unusual for senior Irish clerics to spend time at the papal court, which involved travelling to Avignon or Rome. The two most famous Irish bishops of the fourteenth century, Richard Ledrede and Richard Fitzralph, both lived at the papal court in Avignon for a time. There the prelates were exposed to influences from the wider world. Fitzralph even wrote a critique of the Koran.[221] Others travelled for scholarly reasons – in the thirteenth century one of the chairs of the University of Naples was a man known as

Peter of Ireland.[222] It was missionary clerics, though, and in particular members of the Franciscan order, who were among the greatest travellers in the fourteenth century. In the 1320s Franciscans from Ireland not only travelled to the Jerusalem, then in the hands of the Mamluk Sultanate, but also China, a place to which only a handful of Europeans had ever been.

## Pilgrims

In 1322 two Franciscans, Simon Fitzsimons and Hugo the Illuminator, set out from their friary in Clonmel for the Holy Land. Since the fall of the port of Acre in 1291, the European crusader presence in the Middle East had all but collapsed. In this context Jerusalem was a potentially dangerous destination for Franciscans, but even getting to the Holy Land presented major obstacles. Leaving Ireland in October 1322, the two monks had only reached the city of Chester in England by Easter of the following year, after which their progress improved. They arrived in Paris by the summer of 1323, where Simon, who wrote an extensive account of his journey, was mesmerised by the city. In the 1320s, Paris was one the greatest cities in western Europe and home to at least 100,000 people, dwarfing medieval Dublin, the largest settlement in Ireland. The city astounded the two Anglo-Irish monks. Fitzsimons later described Paris as the 'home and nurse of theological and philosophical science, the mother of the liberal arts, the mistress of justice, the standard of morals, and ... the mirror and lamp of all moral and theological virtues'[223]. By the late summer of 1323 they were travelling down the east coast of the Adriatic Sea, eventually reaching the vast Egyptian city of Alexandria by October. They then continued east to Cairo, where sadly Hugo the Illuminator died. Alone,

Simon successfully completed the remainder of their epic journey, which had taken over a year. While such a journey pushed the bounds of medieval travel, as Simon arrived in Jerusalem, another Irish Franciscan had recently completed another, even more impressive, expedition.

## James of Ireland and the Far East.

Little is known of the Franciscan Jacobus de Hybernia or 'James of Ireland'. He holds the title of almost certainly being the first known Irish person to visit China[224]. This journey was far more difficult than the trip to the Holy Land. He travelled into what was a relatively unknown world when he crossed Asia to what medieval Europeans called Cathay, or as we know it, China. China, even in the fourteenth century, was almost more myth than reality for many Europeans. Indeed, all of eastern Asia had been completely unknown to western Europe up until the previous century. In the early decades of the 1200s the Mongols had unleashed one of the greatest conquests in world history. Having conquered large parts of China, the Middle East and modern Russia, their seemingly invincible forces reached the Danube in eastern Europe by the 1240s. Relatively suddenly Europeans became well acquainted with the eastern Asians and their swords as the Mongols seemed poised to conquer western Europe. The invasion only stopped when the Great Khan Ögedei died in 1241. As succession to the largest Empire in world history was up for grabs, the conquest of the backwater that was medieval Europe was put to one side.

This mysterious army that had nearly conquered Europe made many, including the Pope, inquisitive to say the least. Initially the papacy dispatched John of Plano Carpini to travel to Mongolia to the court of the great Khan, where he arrived in 1246. He was soon followed by missionaries, and in the 1250s William of Rubruck arrived, who hoped to initiate the conversion of the powerful Mongols. It was only after these Franciscans that the famous Marco Polo ventured east, arriving around 1274. Before Polo arrived home in 1295, even more Franciscans were trekking across Asia. They were celebrating modest successes, and before the end of the thirteenth century Giovanni de Monte Corvino became the first Bishop of Beijing. It was in this context that the Franciscan Oderico di Perdione set out east. Although questioned in some quarters, his travelling companion was almost certainly James of Ireland[225] when he left Europe around 1318. The journey they faced was daunting to say the least. While James had no doubt spent months travelling from Ireland to Italy along roads that were at times perilous, he now faced a truly epic journey through what would be at times completely unknown territories. The little if any protection his religious position afforded him in Europe would be meaningless to many they would meet in Asia. They also faced major linguistic problems outside of Europe, where they would encounter languages they had never heard before.

James and Oderico's journey began on well-worn paths through what were the remains of the Byzantine Empire, before making their way to the city of Trebizbond on the south coast of the Black Sea. From there they struck farther east to Tabriz before turning south and making their way to the port of Ormuz on the coast of the Arabian Sea. At Ormuz they took ship to India. Arriving at Thana on the east coast of the subcontinent, the two travellers picked up a macabre cargo – the remains of four martyred Franciscans who had tried to establish a mission. Oderico insisted that they carry the bones with them to ensure they received a proper burial. No doubt both men must have wondered whether they would meet a similar fate as had befallen their brothers in China. Undaunted, they continued by sea to south-east Asia, where the two Franciscans may well have encountered their first Chinese people, and the naval marvels that were the enormous Junks. Junks were Chinese trading vessels that plied the seas in the region. These ships would have astounded both Oderico and James. While large ships in Europe were a few dozen metres in length, Chinese Junks were juggernauts in comparison. The crew and guards alone amounted to a thousand men according to the later Arab traveller Ibn Battuta. Passing by way of Java and Borneo they eventually arrived in the port of Guangzhou on the Pearl River in eastern China. The port amazed the travellers, not only in size but also in terms of goods available. Ginger, an extremely rare and valuable commodity in Europe, was freely available in the markets of the city. Continuing en route to their final destination of Beijing, they encountered the first Franciscan friaries of the east, proof that the previous missionaries' work was somewhat successful. Here they buried the four Franciscans, whose remains they had carried the thousands of miles from Thana. Eventually, after months of further travel within China, they arrived in Beijing, where they met the ailing and aged Bishop Giovanni de Monte Corvino.

Beijing can only have astounded the two Europeans. The city's population was around one million people in the fourteenth century, substantially more than the entire population of medieval Ireland. Famed for its forbidden city, it was the capital of the Mongol Empire ruled over by Buyantu Khan, the great-grandson of the famous Kublai Khan, whom Marco Polo had met several decades earlier. The two monks preached in China for about three years in the mid-1320s before returning to Europe to seek more aid for the missionary project in Asia. En route home they may even have visited the Tibetan capital Lhasa, becoming the first westerners to do so; Oderico di Perdenone later described the Dalai Lama as a form of Pope. Arriving back in Italy in 1330, their account astounded people. Oderico's version of events was transcribed by a fellow Franciscan, William of Sologna, in Padua, and it became second only to the famous *Travels of Marco Polo*. Unsurprisingly the epic journey had taken its toll, and Oderico died the following year, leaving in his will two marks to his travelling companion, James of Ireland. Little is known of James afterwards. While Oderico would gain fame after his account of the journey was transcribed, James was largely forgotten. Whether he returned to Ireland is a mystery. His ultimate mission, which was to convert the Mongol Empire to Christianity, was a failure; by the end of the 1330s it was Islam that was making the greatest inroads.

While James' journey east was unusual in terms of distance, many in medieval Ireland spent large amounts of their lives travelling. For some this was simply repeating relatively short, local journeys within Ireland, while for others like James, Simon Fitzsimons or Hugo the Illuminator, travel brought them to places far from the shores of their home.

# 16

# You're having a laugh?
# Fun in the 'Land of War'

I n 1308, settlements like Newcastle Lyons were gripped with fear of the threat of violence. The nearby Wicklow Mountains rose above the settlement as a constant reminder of the menace they faced. In May 1308, violence had erupted in these mountains when Gaelic Irish rebels had burned the fortress of Castlekevin near Glendalough, and the entire garrison was put to the sword.[226] It was clear that turbulent times lay ahead. Incidents like this had frequently led to widespread violence across the region. Indeed, the settlement of Saggart, scarcely five miles from Newcastle, had for decades been described as being near 'the land of war'[227] – a term that described regions susceptible to attack.

Since 1270, Gaelic Irish attacks on colonial territory had not only increased in frequency, but were also successful. Indeed, by the early fourteenth century, life for colonists was increasingly difficult and dangerous. The fraught nature of life in medieval Ireland was illustrated in a court case in 1312. Several men had crept up on the town of Hugetoun le Rede at night and called aloud, 'Fennok abo'. This was the well-known war cry of the Gaelic Irish O'Tooles, and petrified the residents of the town, who simply fled without an investigation. On this occasion it turned out to be rather opportunistic thieves, who helped themselves to some cheese and chickens.[228] Such a land of war is not an environment in which we can imagine people having fun. Despite living in fear of attack, however, life didn't stop, and people enjoyed themselves as best they could.

## Football

In Newcastle Lyons, during that tense summer of 1308, one of the earliest games of football was recorded in medieval Ireland. The backdrop to the game was an increasingly dire military situation after a major Norman host under John de Wogan was defeated by the Gaelic Irish in the Wicklow Mountains on 8 June. Nonetheless, a few weeks later the inhabitants of the frontier colonial settlement of Newcastle Lyons, who lived within view of the mountains, still organised a ball game on St John's day. This feast day on 24 June was a major event in the medieval calendar, and this game was presumably part of the wider festivities to celebrate the occasion.

While there is little doubt that this was just one of dozens of games being played all across the Vale of Dublin on this feast day, knowledge of this game at Newcastle Lyons has survived due to an unfortunate accident. When the ball came in the direction of John McCorcan, who was 'standing near to watch the game'[229], he and a friend, William Bernard, chased it. Unfortunately, it being fourteenth-century Ireland, McCorcan carried a knife with him, and when he clashed with William 'he wounded [him] in the upper part of his right leg with a knife which pierced its sheath and so injured William'.[230]

Despite this accident, events such as this game highlight the fact that life in medieval Ireland was not an endless story of violence and oppression. When they had the chance, people enjoyed themselves in much the same way as we do today. It is only our perspective from the twenty-first century experience of life in the western hemisphere that makes it hard for us to comprehend how anyone could possibly have fun when surrounded by so much pain, sadness and misery.

People living in the thirteenth and fourteenth centuries saw, and experienced, their world very differently. Terrors such as famine and war were not unusual; not so much temporary mishaps as a matter of their life experience. Even during quite violent periods, people had to get on with their lives, and enjoying themselves was an integral part of that. Having fun was not incompatible with life in a violent society, but rather an important part of it, and contrary to what we might expect they had far more time to enjoy themselves.

## Free Time

The vast majority in medieval society, the peasantry, worked in agriculture. Their calendar was not shaped by a working week of nine to five, Monday to Friday, but instead their time was heavily structured around the seasons. During the harvest season they worked intensely hard, while in winter they had far less to do. While peasants were a wide and varied bunch, this working life left many in Anglo-Norman Ireland with relatively large amounts of spare time. While the free time of peasants in England was constricted by the 100 days of labour each year that most peasants owed to their feudal lords as rents, circumstances were different in Ireland.

Peasants in Ireland generally owed very little labour service to a system most likely initiated to attract colonists from England.[231] This left large amounts of the year free for other tasks, either working on farms during the harvest or ploughing season, or working their own land if they had some. It also left time aside for pastimes and enjoyment. Sports were popular, just as they are today, and the mention of ball games in Newcastle in 1308 was by no means the only mention of such sports.

## Games on the Liffey

In 1338, Dublin experienced an exceptionally cold winter. The harsh weather was marked by a very hard frost and snows, which ground life to a halt, so much so that the River Liffey itself completely froze over. While unusual, this posed a major threat to medieval life; harsh weather damaged crops, which resulted in a serious famine in 1339. Nevertheless, to mark this unusual occurrence the city's population had a festival of sorts on the ice, where they not only 'leaped and danced' but also made 'fires of turf and of wood on the ice', where they broiled herrings.[232] Dangerous as all this may sound, the frozen Liffey also supported a game of ball![233]

While football was popular, the Norman colonists in the fourteenth century appeared to have played a form of hurling, or possibly hockey. This appears to have been very popular, so much so that it was prohibited in the famous Statutes of Kilkenny in the 1360s. One statute outlined the problems they had with a game '*which men call horlings, with great sticks and a ball upon the ground, from which great evils and maims have arisen*'[234]. This appears to have been an effort to promote archery in a colonial society that seemed like it was going to collapse in the face of ever-increasing Gaelic attacks in the late fourteenth century. The 'horlings' mentioned above was not the only sport banned for this reason; a later statute also banned bowling for similar reasons.[235]

There were also other outdoor pursuits, many of which would have a resonance today. While medieval cities were smaller than modern cities, they were far more cramped and smelly. Unsurprisingly, there are several references to people enjoying festivities or 'playing' in the fields outside cities.[236] Escaping the pungent aromas of cesspits, rotting food and the body odour of thousands of people in the height of summer can have been no less enjoyable than escaping a modern city today. As usual, we get our record of such activities from events that went wrong. In 1209, such an event was recorded when scores of Dubliners were killed at Cullenswood (Ranelagh) while enjoying a festival in what was then countryside when the Gaelic Irish launched a surprise attack.

## Drinking

While medieval pastimes may appear to have been wholesome and healthy, the people of the late Middle Ages enjoyed many unhealthy pastimes, just like us. It is oft repeated how problematic alcohol consumption is in Ireland today, and this was no less the case in medieval times. Consuming alcohol was a very popular form of socialising. Taverns and inns were popular, with frequent mentions in surviving documents. In 1367, the Archbishop of Dublin, Thomas Minot, complained that people did not engage in religious activities on feast days but instead spent the days in 'taverns and drunkenness and other illicit acts of pleasure'.[237]

Unfortunately, in a world where people carried weapons such as knives and swords as a matter of course, socialising in a heavily inebriated state could have disastrous consequences. At a court sitting in 1300 in Kilmallock, the Justiciar heard how Hugh de Mora drew his sword in a tavern and struck a woman, wounding her in the head, before Martin Kadigan brought him to task. Although the case is ambiguous, it appears that Hugh may just have been drunk in drawing his sword and had accidentally struck the woman. There was no such ambiguity about Martin Kadigan, who maimed de Mora with his axe in response.[238]

While entertainment and pastimes no doubt provided relief during what was at times a harsh existence, the all-pervasive violence that permeated society also heavily influenced pastimes. The great class divides of the era were starkly apparent in these pursuits.

## Archery and Hunting

Archery was also a common medieval pastime. In February 1311, a court case revealed that shepherds practised archery to hone a skill that they would, some day, potentially use to save their lives. Unfortunately, on this occasion a certain Mabilla was sitting near the target. The shepherds asked her to move, but after Mabilla refused, they resumed their practice, regardless of the threat posed to her safety. The result was all too predictable. One of the shepherds, John Clement, struck Mabilla in the head with an arrow, which was caught by the wind and had blown in her direction.[239] Despite the fact that they were using a blunted arrow, the wound was fatal.

The aristocracy took such martial pastimes to a different level entirely. Aside from the jousting tournaments, hunting was a far more common pursuit. There are several references to the deer parks and hunting grounds that they owned. These were vast private lands where no one else was allowed to hunt without permission from the relevant noble, which ensured a plentiful supply of stock to hunt. Hunting, while it may have on occasion produced food, was far more focussed on the martial rituals involved in chasing and killing beasts. While the more violent forms of medieval pastimes have thankfully waned and become increasingly obsolete, the medieval interest in performance and drama has survived the test of time.

## Drama, Songs and Story.

In a world where there was scarcely any media, let alone a mass media or social media, poems and stories were popular. Naturally, these reflected the world they were composed in. Songs such as 'The Maid in the Moorland' recounted women's understandable frustrations about being married to men who could be up to twice their age. Likewise, in an era that glorified war, this subject was to be found in the poems of the age. One of the earliest surviving epics from Anglo-Norman Ireland, commonly known as 'The Song of Dermot and the Earl', is a story that retells the conquest of Ireland by Strongbow and his Anglo-Norman followers. These stories were the television, radio or YouTube of the era, filling the void on many dark winter nights.

Public performances of dramas also entertained people of the medieval world and, like our contemporaries, playwrights of the era tried to analyse the world as it happened around them. The earliest surviving text from Anglo-Norman Ireland that was the basis for a theatrical performance is *The Pride of Life*, which originates from around 1350.[240] Possibly written immediately after the Black Death, in a period in which people were only too aware of their own mortality, the drama tries to give structure to a chaotic world that had suffered immensely.[241] The play, unsurprisingly, has strong themes of immortality, mortality and the afterlife. Such forms of entertainment were no doubt important ways for people to deal with the trauma of living through these events in a more relaxed setting. Where exactly such plays were performed is not certain. By 1506, plays were performed in Dublin on a stage erected at Hoggen Green (College Green).[242] Hoggen Green was also where other public spectacles were staged in the fourteenth century, including certain executions, so it is likely that it hosted these early performances as well.

Fun and entertainment in medieval Ireland not only existed, but formed an essential part of life, allowing people to escape from, and deal with, what was at times a very difficult world around them. There is no doubt that there is some truth to the stereotypical world we imagine, where, due to brutality, there was little to celebrate. In 1315–18, during the depths of famine and the Bruce invasion, few could have had the energy to play games, the money to drink in taverns or the inclination to watch plays, but such times were transient. Such extreme events, while frequent, did pass.

# 17

# John Clyn: Living and Dying in Extraordinary Times

When the Franciscan Friar John Clyn died in 1349, he had lived through an exceptional period. Growing up during the famines of 1295 and 1310, his family's wealth shielded him from the worst excesses of starvation. As a young man he witnessed the Bruce invasion of 1315, when neither rank nor title was a guarantee of safety.

He then endured renewed aristocratic civil war in the 1320s, when the de Burghs and Le Poers fought the Butlers and Fitzgeralds in a devastating conflict. Finally, in his later years, the Black Death – the worst outbreak of disease in recorded human history – struck Ireland in 1348. These strange and dangerous times saw some take advantage of the violent and precarious world in which they lived. Amid the chaos of the early fourteenth century, Richard de Burgh, the Earl of Ulster, became one of the most powerful aristocrats in north-western Europe. Later in the century, James Butler, the Second Earl of Ormond, was another who was able to excel in these times of crisis, to his and his family's advantage.

There were also those who failed to meet the challenge of such times. Richard de Burgh's son William, his successor as Earl of Ulster, was assassinated within seven years of assuming his title after incurring the wrath of his relatives. In this age of extremes, John Clyn was neither a great failure nor a great success. Although educated (a rare asset in the fourteenth century), he failed to make a mark on the chaotic world around him.

The final year of his life was, however, to see a radical change in Ireland. When the Black Death – the bubonic plague that killed almost half the population – devastated Ireland in 1348, this aged Franciscan friar penned one of the most vivid accounts of the terror wrought by the outbreak. This succinct account would make him one of the most noted figures of fourteenth-century Ireland. After a life of mediocrity, his writing in late 1348 and 1349 granted him immortality, so much so that over six centuries after his death there is scarcely a book written on the Black Death that doesn't mention him.

John Clyn was born into an Anglo-Norman family during the 1280s[243] in north Kilkenny. Although his family was relatively wealthy, they left little historical trace save the place name: Clinstown[244]. Surviving the terrors of the Bruce invasion when much of south Kilkenny was devastated, Clyn joined the Franciscan order and was educated by them.

Cowled in their grey habits, the Franciscans were sworn to a life of poverty and preached among the wider population, often proselytising to the poor. In the later thirteenth century the order's strict vows of poverty were relaxed, and they accepted endowments of land in Ireland by 1297[245]. In the following decades, further enrichment created tensions, factions within the order arguing as to what exactly their commitment to a life of poverty meant.

In a society torn by tensions between the Gaelic Irish and Anglo-Normans, the order could not escape this turmoil. In 1291, at a meeting of Franciscans held in Cork, several friars were reportedly killed in a fracas between Anglo-Norman and Gaelic Irish friars. Despite living through such tumultuous times, John Clyn never held extreme opinions on either issue. Along with many colonists, he was deeply suspicious of the Gaelic Irish, but he never voiced the same virulent hatred toward them as some of his fellow Franciscans. Perhaps it was due to his uncontroversial nature that he was able to rise within the Franciscan order; by the 1330s he had been guardian of Franciscan friaries at both Carrick-on-Suir and Kilkenny.

Despite his position of authority, John Clyn was by no means the most well-known Franciscan in Ireland, or even his own diocese. Through Clyn's life, Kilkenny was dominated by the Franciscan Richard Ledrede, the Bishop of Ossory who conducted some of Ireland's earliest heresy and witchcraft trials (see chapter 13, p.87). Even after Ledrede was exiled from Ireland during the 1330s and 1340s for political intrigues, Clyn appears to have made little advancement. He is not mentioned in any political or historical record other than the one written by Clyn himself. His greatest achievement appears to have been his chronicle, a history of Kilkenny he compiled after 1333[246]. Unsurprisingly, given the world in which he lived, this chronicle became a catalogue of local feuds and power politics peppered with ecclesiastical history and reports from Europe.

By the 1340s John Clyn had reached the age of sixty, almost twice the average age of many of the poor of Kilkenny to whom he preached. Given what he had already lived through, Clyn could hardly have expected any great changes in his remaining years. In 1348, however, life was radically transformed. The catalyst for this almost revolutionary change was the arrival of the Black Death, after which nothing would ever be the same again.

In the summer of 1348, the most unusual of battles was underway in Dublin and Drogheda. It did not involve swords, shields or arrows; the aggressors were small human-biting fleas. While tiny, these fleas, or rather the bacteria they hosted, caused more destruction than any medieval war ever could have. Infected with the bacteria *yersinia pestis*, the fleas spread a disease known to history as the Black Death or the bubonic plague. In the fourteenth century it was aptly and unsurprisingly named 'the great mortality' after it killed over one third of the European population between 1347 and 1349.

Depending on the form it took, victims developed large buboes (swollen lymph nodes) in their armpits or groin, some spat or coughed blood, while the skin darkened and the patient burned with fever. What was an excruciating death could come in a matter days or even hours. It spread at alarming rate, travelling from Marseille to Ireland in around twelve months. After gaining a foothold in the major ports on the east coast, the disease's progress dramatically slowed. In the first six months it appears to have been confined to a region between Dublin and Drogheda. Nearly eighty years of warfare had made the main thoroughfare from Dublin to Kilkenny and the other Norman colonial territory in the south and south-west almost untraversable by regular traffic. While this hamstrung daily life, in 1348 it prevented the spread of the Black Death overland.

Nonetheless, fear of the plague and the inevitability of its spread across Ireland provoked terror among the population. In Kilkenny, Friar John Clyn began to document the impact this plague fear was having on wider society in his chronicle. In autumn 1348, before plague ever reached Kilkenny, the population were clearly and understandably beginning to panic.

Clyn noted how thousands flocked to a holy well at St Moling on the Barrow River. Situated twenty miles south-east of Kilkenny, the well's association with a saint renowned for healing attracted multitudes, who Clyn reported came 'in fear of plague that then prevailed without measure'[247]. This panic was fuelled by reports from Dublin and Drogheda about conditions in these plague-ridden towns. Clyn's haunting description of the settlements being 'wasted of inhabitants and men'[248] was an indication of what was in store for the population of Kilkenny.

Having no understanding of what the plague was or how it developed, many believed it was the harbinger of the end of the world. Clyn himself recalled the apocalyptic prediction, the Prophecy of Tripoli. Despite being an obvious reworking of an earlier prophecy relating to the Crusades, its prediction of famine and war concluding with a line about the arrival of the Antichrist must have had resonance.

While it obviously constituted a major event in history, many contemporary chronicles are strangely silent, scarcely mentioning anything other than the plague's arrival. This is probably indicative of the wider societal collapse that took hold in many areas as the population was decimated. John Clyn reacted differently, continuing through the crisis to write his chronicle documenting the disease's advance.

While Kilkenny remained free from the disease through most of 1348, disturbing news about the effects of the plague continued to arrive in the town. Clyn reported that twenty-five Franciscans had died in Drogheda, and in Dublin a further twenty-three friars had succumbed. These statistics were akin to a death sentence for a Franciscan like Clyn: where it struck, the plague was killing the vast majority of Franciscans. Although the Franciscan houses in Dublin and Drogheda were probably among the largest of the thirty-three friaries in Ireland[249], this was still an extremely high death rate; the average community consisted of around thirteen friars.[250]

Fear of death began to encroach upon every aspect of life. While commerce continued, people displayed an increasing awareness of their mortality. In November 1348, Patrick and Johanna de la Freyne, friends of Clyn, bought lands in Carlow. The deed of transfer contained detailed provisions of what was to happen to the lands should Patrick and Johanna die[251]. The de la Freynes also included a caveat, detailing to whom the lands were to pass if their children and their children's heirs were also to perish. While terms like this were not unheard of in the fourteenth century, this caveat must have had particular resonance in November 1348. The complete extinction of entire families was a distinct possibility once the plague struck a region.

In what must have felt like a negation of all hope, the Black Death took hold in Kilkenny around Christmas 1348. Its passage was most likely on board ship up the River Nore from the busy port of New Ross.[252] John Clyn reported the morbid events that unfolded in Kilkenny. Eight members of the Dominican order in Kilkenny died within two and half months. Outside the religious institutions, the town's population was decimated, Clyn observing that there 'was scarcely a house in which only one died but commonly man and wife with their children and family going one way, namely, crossing to death'[253].

Unfortunately, Clyn failed to reveal how this turmoil affected daily life in Kilkenny, but judging from contemporary accounts across Europe, society more or less broke down. Giovanni Boccaccio's book *The Decameron* details how the population of Florence reacted during the outbreak there. He observed three distinct reactions.[254] The first course of resort, self-exclusion from society, was the most effective. This saw people locking themselves away for the duration of the plague. This quarantine was only really available to the rich, who could retreat to their country castles to avoid contact. The poor, living in narrow, crowded streets in small houses, had no such hope of escape in this manner.

The second reaction was a timeless one. Boccaccio revealed that many sought to 'carouse and make merry and go about singing and playing games and satisfy ones appetite in every possible way'[255]. This is a common reaction throughout history when people face impending disaster. There are twentieth-century parallels for such behaviour: a similar attitude prevailed in Berlin as the Soviet Army approached the city in 1945, and tales of brutal acts being perpetrated in eastern Prussia terrified the population. In fourteenth-century Europe, while the agent of terror did not have a human face, the population was no less fearful.

The final response Boccaccio described was that of a middle course between these extremes, where people, in the face of relentless and ever encroaching death, simply continued with their lives as best they could[256]. John Clyn fell into this latter category. Surrounded by death, he nevertheless maintained the resolve to continue documenting the events. Of course, he was by no means the only one in Kilkenny to hold his nerve. In a similar fashion to the means by which men like Richard de Burgh had taken advantage of earlier crises, in 1349 there were those who were only too willing to take advantage of the Black Death.

William Coterel was from Kells, a settlement south of Kilkenny. Throughout the fourteenth century the Coterel family had expanded their influence in Kells and the surrounding countryside by purchasing large amounts of land through the crisis-ridden decades of famine and war. They were particularly active in the decade after the Fitzgeralds burned the town in 1327 in their wars against the le Poers[257]. By 1337 William Coterel had purchased at least eleven plots in and around Kells alone[258]. In early 1349, as plague swept through the region, the Coterels again took advantage of the crisis. In January, while the plague raged, William Coterel bought land near Kells from David March[259]. A few months later, two other members of the family, Catherine and Christiana Coterel, bought a further eight acres[260]. While no record of land prices survive, the drastic fall in population and uncertainty about the future undoubtedly reduced the demand for property and, presumably, the price followed suit. As others focused on the enjoyment of what they feared were their last days, the Coterels, being a family who had accrued property through numerous crises, realised the potential of the chaotic events.

In the Franciscan friary in nearby Kilkenny, John Clyn was also not overtaken by events, as evidenced by his writing. Yet, as the death toll mounted and up to half of Kilkenny's population of at least 4,000 people[261] perished, he believed that humanity was facing extinction. He finished his account of the plague with the poignant words: 'I am leaving parchment for the work to continue if, by chance in the future a man should remain surviving, and anyone of the race of Adam should be able to escape this plague and [live] to continue this work [I have] commenced'[262]. In the following months the plague eventually subsided, running its course after around six months. While Clyn never revealed losses at his Franciscan friary in Kilkenny, the deaths of the custos, guardian and lector at the friary in Nenagh were indicative of the trauma he endured.

Having suffered the horrors of the great mortality, the post-plague world offered little for survivors. Violence and upheaval dominated a world with an uncertain future. The plague had barely subsided when Clyn noted the death of his close friend Fulk de la Freyne, who was assassinated in June 1349 by the Gaelic Irish. Indeed, the Gaelic Irish were left in a stronger position following the plague as they had not suffered as much as the Anglo-Normans; living on poorer lands, they were often on high ground where the plague bacteria could not thrive.

Numerically far stronger than they had been previously, they now enjoyed a distinct advantage, and the Anglo-Normans in Kilkenny were clearly insecure. The most powerful figure in the region, James Butler, the Earl of Ormond, entered into an unprecedented six treaties and indentures with the local Gaelic Irish in the following decade[263]. This temporary tactical change, toward conciliation rather than war, was essentially forced on the likes of Butler. Regardless, the decade following the Black Death was one of hardship in general. As the poor in society demanded higher wages, the rich responded with force and coercive laws (see chapter 7, p.52).

The experience of plague also changed society in more fundamental ways. Having survived what seemed to be an apocalypse, this event transformed the way in which people perceived themselves. In the early 1350s the clergy began to argue against what they saw as rising selfishness and greed[264].

John Clyn did not live to see these events, although he does appear to have survived the plague and reported briefly on the aftermath; corn increased in price, and imported goods such as pepper became incredibly expensive. This surge in price was due to the detrimental impact plague had on coastal communities and mariners[265]

– there were simply fewer people to sail ships and import goods. Writing what would be his final entry, he turned to more personal matters, reporting the death of his friend Fulk de la Friegne.

What happened to John Clyn next is unclear, but the chronicle remains silent until another scribe later writes 'here it seems the author died'[266]. In a harsh twist of fate, it is likely that Clyn died from natural causes only weeks after surviving the plague. On his death he was still a minor figure, even in Kilkenny. In later centuries, however, it was Clyn's clarity in chaos, and the writing from that brief period in 1348–49, that would grant him fame and, in a manner, immortality. While by no means the most detailed account of the time, his manuscript is one of the few written during the actual events themselves. Many of the others, such as Boccaccio's *The Decameron*, were written in later years as authors looked back with hindsight. Clyn, of course, could not have this perspective. His unusual ability to continue writing amidst the chaos and death gives us a unique window into medieval Ireland, and indeed Europe, during one of its greatest crises.

# 18

# Fires: A Medieval Tsunami

Watching the city you grew up in burn to the ground is something that is thankfully unimaginable in modern Ireland. This luxury, however, was not something our ancestors enjoyed. On the night of 9 June 1301, an inferno ripped through the heart of medieval Dublin, destroying a large section of the city[267]. The neighbourhood between the two great stone structures that dominated the skyline, Dublin Castle and Christchurch Cathedral, was reduced to ashes. Among the buildings destroyed was the parish church of St Werburgh's. The social cost was immense as homes, property and possessions of many of the city's residents were consumed by the intensity of the conflagration. In a society with no insurance policies, such people lost everything.

## Dublin and Fire Laws

Devastating as it was, fires of this magnitude were by no means unique in medieval cities. The threat of fire was part and parcel of urban life. Charred and burned shells of buildings were a common sight in towns, testaments to fires long past, often remaining derelict for years. With these constant reminders of the dangers posed by fire, urban authorities took this potential hazard very seriously. In Dublin, laws were enacted to contain the threat of fire whereby each person was fully responsible for their own house. No mercy was shown, even when fires broke out accidentally, and punishments were severe, even for the most minor of infringements. In the laws and usages of Dublin compiled in the early fourteenth century, a householder who suffered the misfortune of having an uncontrolled fire inside their house was still liable for a fine of £1. This was a considerable amount of money at the time, far more than rural labourers earned in a year. If the fire was more serious and flames were visible from without the house, the fine was doubled to £2. In a situation where a domestic fire resulted in the burning of an entire street, a very distinct possibility, the person liable could be executed. The law stated that the householder in question was to 'be arrested, cast into the middle of the fire'![268] Should they survive the wrath of their neighbours, they were liable for the fine of £5. In Kilkenny, a similar situation prevailed, where to 'threaten ... burning a house or anything else'[269] was specifically mentioned as a crime. While medieval authorities took punishment very seriously, they were equally vigilant. Many towns had a city watch by the early fourteenth century, which was a forerunner to a police force. When such a body was established in Kilkenny in the 1350s, the authorities noted that a watch was not only to keep a lookout for thieves, but also to watch for fires.[270] While these laws and ordinances may seem extreme, it is an understatement to say they were introduced for good reason. When fires caught hold in towns, the result was nothing short of catastrophic. Medieval cities were veritable tinderboxes, largely constructed of flammable material, and one careless act could be disastrous. To make matters worse, the city streets were rarely planned. They were more often than not narrow, claustrophobic, crowded, winding lanes with houses packed densely together with little thought for safety. Merchants crammed these narrow thoroughfares with various goods. In Kilkenny in 1337, a law referred to the practice of 'heap[ing] of grain, turf or firewood in the street'.[271] In Dublin, numerous laws referred to the stalls along the streets and to the practice of women sitting along the pavement with baskets selling goods. If the buildings on the side of a street caught fire, it would not have taken long for flames to spread through the cluttered streets, which were packed full of material that served as perfect kindling.

## Dwellings

To make matters worse, inside the medieval city dwellings the fire hearth was surrounded by flammable material; not only was the furniture made from timber, but in many cases the walls and ceilings were constructed from wattle, a material that burned easily. If this wasn't enough highly combustible material, dried reeds were frequently used to line the floors. Even when the more dangerous open hearths were replaced by enclosed fireplaces and chimneys from around 1300 onwards, this did little to curtail the dangers of fire catching hold. Many of these houses doubled as workshops for cottage industries, where safety was not a major priority. There are many court records that mention children playing around fires. In Cork in 1313, a four-year-old child, Robert son of Thomas, was playing in a house where mead was being brewed when he accidentally fell into a pan of hot water and honey, after which he died[272]. Even in summer, when people had less need for indoor fires, the dry weather presented its own problems. As the timber frames of the houses dried out, it served to heighten their combustibility. The development of stone houses did little to improve the dangers faced from fire. They still had roofs made from thatch, composed of layers of dried vegetation. In hot summers the thatch dried out to the point of merely needing a spark to set it ablaze. Facing these multiple risks, as we saw, the medieval authorities did their best to try and manage their warren-like cities with severe fines. They also went as far as prohibiting fires in certain locations, which were deemed too risky. In Dublin in the early fourteenth century, a law was enacted stating 'No warehouse less than ten feet in width shall have a fire'[273].

## The Great Fires of Dublin

No matter how much they tried, it was impossible to stop fires breaking out, and these could be utterly devastating. Dublin, medieval Ireland's most populous settlement, experienced several fires during its history, some of which nearly destroyed the entire city. While Dublin had experienced devastation in military campaigns from its earliest days in the ninth century, one of the first recorded accidental fires dates from 1192, when it was recorded that 'the city of Dublin was burnt'[274]. Although medieval chroniclers are renowned for hyperbole, the suggestion that the whole settlement was burned is entirely plausible. In the late twelfth century, Dublin was largely constructed from timber; there were very few stone buildings aside from the ecclesiastical structures in the city at this stage. Through the thirteenth century Dublin grew in size and scale, and by the closing decades of the century the increased population of around 10,000 people were living in a very confined space. Despite there being far more stone buildings, the overcrowding and cramped conditions led to several major fires.

The year 1283 marked the beginning of a truly disastrous thirty-four year period for Dublin. Three days into the new year, Christchurch Cathedral, one of the biggest buildings inside the city walls, was very badly damaged in a conflagration. An annalist recorded 'the city of Dublin was in part burnt, and the belfry of St Trinity Church in Dublin'[275]. The charred and burnt belfry would have dominated the medieval skyline as the tallest structure in the city, serving as a stark reminder to the dangers posed by fire, as if one were needed. This was followed by the St Werburgh's fire in 1301, which devastated the heart of the medieval city again. Scarcely had Dublin recovered than yet another blaze broke out in 1304, when 'A great part of Dublin was burnt with the Bridge street with a good part of the quay'[276]. This fire appears to have been incredibly intense, as it spread across the River Liffey, consuming the Dominican church and a large part of the monastery, which were situated on the north bank of the river where the Four Courts stand today. Recovery after these fires could take years. The gate and wall at Bridge Street was described as having been burned and knocked down after the fire of 1304, and was still in disrepair as late as 1308[277].

Incidentally, it was these repairs that became the centre of one the greatest tax scams in Dublin's history. Geoffrey Morton, a one-time mayor of the city, inveigled the king and the people of Dublin into giving him hundreds of pounds of taxes under the pretence of carrying out repairs needed after the fire. He used the money to renovate and expand his house, which only served to undermine the city defences even further! This only served to slow down the restoration needed after the 1304 fire. Even as late as 1311, another defensive tower on the wall (Isolde's Tower) and the city quays further east were still described as ruinous[278]. While this was unquestionably a serious incident that scarred the city for years, it was sadly only a prelude to the worst inferno in Dublin's history, which occurred in 1317. This would not only be Dublin's greatest fire, but also the most unusual one. It started amid exceptional circumstances, whereby, in spite of all their laws and regulations, the citizens of Dublin intentionally set their own city on fire on 24 February 1317.

## The Great Fire of 1317

By early 1317, Dublin was enduring one of its darkest periods. Famine had raged through Ireland since 1315, and cannibalism was widely reported. To make matters worse, in 1315 Edward Bruce, the brother of the King of Scotland, invaded Ireland. In the following years, vast tracts of land across Ulster and Leinster were destroyed in several military campaigns waged by Bruce and the Anglo-Normans. Remarkably, Dublin managed to avoid direct attack in the first two years of war. By late 1316 the conflict was approaching a stalemate, and in an effort to break the deadlock the King of Scotland, Robert the Bruce, arrived in Ireland in person with a large army. While the Bruce's armies had previously avoided getting bogged down in protracted sieges, in February 1317 they marched on Dublin, hoping to land a decisive blow against the Norman colony by capturing this key settlement. Understandably, fear and panic gripped the city. St Saviour's priory, damaged in the fire of 1304, was pulled down, and the stone used to beef up the city defences. On 23 February 1317, the Bruce's force arrived on the north bank of the river. They immediately stormed Castleknock Castle and set up camp north west of Dublin. With no hope of a relieving army arriving in time, the population began to prepare for the worst. With fears that the Scots would storm the city, the following day attention began to focus on the vast suburb to the west of Dublin around Thomas Street. It was feared that the Scots would use the houses to provide cover for a potential assault on the city walls. Amid fear and desperation, the townspeople set the suburb alight to deny the Scots this cover, but unsurprisingly the inferno was soon out of control. The blaze quickly burned house after house, sweeping through not only the suburb of St Thomas, but engulfing the other suburb of St Patrick's further to the east. Before it had burned out, the conflagration had consumed most buildings south of the city walls. The destruction even spread as far east as the exchequer building, which stood on the corner where Exchequer Street and George's Street meet today. Miraculously, the population within the walls managed to stop the blaze crossing the moat between the city and the suburbs. Had this happened, the entire city would have burned to the ground. Nonetheless, the damage to Dublin was catastrophic, being valued shortly afterwards at £10,000[279]. Even in the economic heyday of the colony, long gone by 1317, the exchequer had never taken in much more than £9,000[280] in one year.

It appears that the vast majority of the houses in the suburbs were destroyed. The citizens later argued that the city rent of £133 paid annually to the Crown needed to be reduced down to £33[281], indicating that as much as 75% of the city's properties had been damaged.

The impact of this fire marked the start of a long decline of medieval Dublin. In 1326, much of the suburbs were still in ruins. In the streets surrounding St Patrick's Cathedral it seems that over a third of the houses were vacant. In a valuation of the property there belonging to the archbishop, rents on New Street fell from over fifty-seven shillings to just over thirty-two shillings because the rest of the street was said to be in 'waste'. On nearby Patrick's Street, a similar situation prevailed.[282] The suburbs struggled to recover in the following decades. In 1343, the Thomas Street area 'was casually burnt with fire'[283] on St Valentine's Day. Five years after this fire, the population of Dublin dropped sharply in 1348 during the Black Death, and the need to rebuild suburbs dropped significantly, there being less demand for houses.

While fire would pose a great threat to Dublin for centuries, it was the great fire of 1317 that had wrought the greatest havoc and destruction. In 1610 John Speed drew an early map of the city, which revealed a Dublin scarcely larger than it had been prior to the great fire of 1317. This starkly illustrated how fire was not only part of the dangers of life in a medieval city, but it could be a crucial factor in how modern cities developed.

# 19

# Women and Warfare: Thieves, Spies and Rebels

$\mathfrak{E}$ dmund Butler, the Justiciar of Ireland, returned to Dublin in January 1316 having presided over the latest military disaster to hit in the Norman Colony in Ireland. Since 26 May 26 1315, a Scots army had invaded Ireland and rampaged across the island. The conflict was dominated by stereotypical medieval battles with heavy cavalry charges, archers and foot soldiers. Numerous towns and castles had been sacked, most notably Dundalk, while large tracts of farmland had been burned. In September and December the Scots had defeated Anglo-Norman armies led by the Earl of Ulster and Roger Mortimer respectively.

In January, Butler had himself mobilised an army, which appeared to have gained the upper hand. The Scots were weary, having been on the move for months. Butler, on the other hand, had gathered what could be described as the pride of the Anglo-Norman nobility. Maurice Fitzgerald, the later Earl of Desmond; John Fitzthomas, the future Earl of Kildare; and John le Poer, the Baron of Dunhill, amongst others, were marshalled in the upper Barrow Valley, where they shadowed the Scots. When they joined in battle at

Ardscull outside Athy on 26 January, the result was an embarrassing calamity. The Scots held the battlefield, but not through a military victory: instead, Butler's army appears to have broken up amid internal squabbles.

On returning to Dublin he found little respite. Although the conflict was only six months old, the city bore all the hallmarks of war. The church of St Mary del Dam was in ruins, having been pulled down the previous December in order to use the stone to patch up the city defences in case of a Scots siege. To the south of the city, however, the Anglo-Normans faced a very different type of military problem, but one that nonetheless posed a great threat to Dublin. The entire Anglo-Norman colony in south Dublin and east Wicklow was in danger of collapse under the increasing ferocity of Gaelic Irish raids and attacks.

Fighting the Gaelic Irish in this region was unimaginably different to the battles they had lost against the Scots armies rampaging across Ireland. Rarely if ever did the Gaelic Irish in Wicklow draw up on a battlefield to face down a Norman army. Instead they launched night-time raids, attacked isolated garrisons and stole what they could. After nearly four and half decades of this type of conflict, which bore the hallmarks of guerrilla warfare, the Anglo-Norman colonists in the Wicklow Mountains appeared to be on their last legs. In February 1316 they had arrived in Dublin begging Butler for military aid.

Hugh Lawless, one of the leading colonists in the region, vividly described a society on the verge of collapse. The colonists were only hanging on by a thread, and 'by malice and wantonness of the Irish of the mountains, felons of the king, they have been expelled and removed from many of their fortresses, manors and houses'[284]. He went on to depict the increasingly siege-like existence they endured in the coastal plain of East Wicklow. In a haunting portrayal of life, he described how they were now reduced to living in 'a confined and narrow part of the country' hemmed in by the sea on one side and the mountains on the other[285]. He also recalled how many settlers had been killed by what he called 'Irish felons'[286] and that they only survived 'by the will of those Irishmen'. Lawless was describing a society that was turning into a perpetual nightmare of attacks for the colonists, where year by year life was increasingly intolerable.

What made this conflict most difficult was that there were no clear battle lines. While many of the Gaelic Irish lived in the mountains, effectively outside Norman control, others lived in the frontier colonial settlements. In this world, the male-dominated battlefield disappeared, and was replaced to a certain extent by struggles in communities where there was little to distinguish civilians from soldiers. Women were directly involved in the conflict, and many women were executed for their role in Gaelic Irish advances in the early fourteenth century.

The crisis faced by Hugh Lawless was not unique to East Wicklow; a similar process was underway in many territories surrounding the Wicklow Mountains. From 1309 onwards the O'Byrnes began to threaten northern Carlow[287], which took the form of raids, robberies and murders rather than open conflict, and here women were directly involved in what was a very different form of warfare. In December 1311, William and Tadg Octouthy were convicted of killing Geoffrey le Lang and stealing sixteen cows and forty sheep from him in Carlow. After the two men were found guilty of killing an Anglo-Norman colonist, they were unsurprisingly both sentenced to death.

However, further court cases revealed the true extent of this type of warfare, with numerous women implicated in the raid. Baloch Occothy was convicted of giving the brothers shelter and fined forty pence.[288] Even more serious charges were levelled against Fynyna and Isabella Octouthy, the thieves' mother and sister, when they were hauled before the same court.

The two women were charged with direct involvement. They had not only given them shelter, but they also had 'art and part'[289] in their robberies. Both women were shown no leniency, and also received death sentences. Fynyna, the mother, was to be hanged immediately, while Isabella had to endure an unusually prolonged sentence. As she was pregnant by her husband Thomas de Valle, she was not hanged but instead recommitted to gaol, where she was to give birth to her child.[290] It was only then that she was to face the noose.

Knowledge of colonial territory was crucial for raids, resulting in numerous women paying the ultimate price for spying on the Norman settlements in which they lived and relaying information back to their Gaelic Irish relatives. One person who lived in a world with such divided loyalties was Grace O'Toole. She had married a colonist Andrew le Deveneys sometime before 1305, although she was a member of the O'Toole family who had been to the forefront of attacks on the colony since the 1270s. Such mixed marriages were not unusual; indeed as people lived side by side in communities it was almost inevitable. While it appears that Grace moved to and lived in colonial territory, she also remained in contact with her family in the mountains. This unique position saw her frequently act as a go-between for the colonists and the Gaelic Irish.

In 1305, Grace and her husband Andrew were accused of providing aid to the servant of the felon David O'Toole. After facing a jury they were acquitted, and it was noted that Grace often went 'to the parts of the mountains to see and search for cattle carried off by her race'[291]. Grace, however, was also living through a period where the struggle in east Wicklow was growing increasingly bitter. In 1308 the Anglo-Norman Settlement at Castlekevin was burned and the entire garrison slaughtered. In response, Walter McWalter O'Toole was captured, taken to Dublin, tied to a horse and dragged through the streets. This journey ended at the city gallows, where he was hanged.

While Grace appears to have stayed in contact with her family through this period, her role as a conciliator changed. In 1318, as the situation across the Mountains was growing increasingly dire for the colonists, Grace was hauled before the courts again. This time she was accused of spying, and as a result of her activities 'the men of Saggart were robbed by the Irish of the mountains of diverse goods'[292]. Whether she was guilty of spying all along, or perhaps her attitude to the Norman colonists was changed by the violent situation, we will never know, but she received no mercy. While it is understandable that many Gaelic Irish women were implicated in these activities, however, there were also more unusual cases involving Anglo-Norman women such as Isabella Cadel, who spied for Gaelic Irish rebels.

## Anglo-Norman Spies

While Wicklow was one of the most volatile regions in Ireland in the early fourteenth century, it was matched by the increasingly complex and bitter struggle that engulfed the midlands, where Isabella Cadel lived — a region that had never been truly conquered by the Normans. By the late thirteenth century, two Norman lords, John Fitzthomas and Piers de Bermingham, struggled to control the midlands against encroachments from the Gaelic Irish, largely based in the Slieve Bloom Mountains. The conflict was a shifting series of accords where allies turned on each other at an alarming rate, making for strange coalitions of convenience. For example, in 1295 the Lord of Offaly John Fitzthomas had worked with the Gaelic Irish O'Dempseys to attack the Anglo-Norman town of Kildare, thoroughly pillaging the settlement to the tune of £1,000[293].

It was in this world of unpredictable friends and lethal enemies that Isabella Cadel was born. Her father, William, was a powerful figure. He was a close ally of the Lord of Offaly, John Fitzthomas,[294] and had served as Seneschal of Carlow and Kildare in the late 1270s[295]. Sometime prior to 1302, Isabella was married to Diarmait O'Dempsey, a long-standing Gaelic ally of Fitzthomas and Cadel. William Cadel had led a Norman army to protect the O'Dempseys when the other Gaelic Irish families in the region revolted in the 1270s[296]. Isabella's marriage was no doubt an attempt to cement this alliance.

Unfortunately for Isabella, political relations in the midlands became increasingly strained in the early fourteenth century. In 1298 there were notable attacks by the Gaelic Irish, while in 1303 John Fitzthomas and Piers de Bermingham both had to withdraw from the Irish army travelling to fight in Scotland[297] due to the threat of violence. As the region destabilised and tensions heightened, Isabella was drawn into active participation.

In 1302, she and a servant Fynewell found themselves journeying deep into the Slieve Bloom Mountains to meet Gaelic Irish rebels. For the two women this journey involved traversing what was some of the most dangerous territory in medieval Ireland. When warfare had broken out in 1295, the violence across the midlands had been horrific. On that occasion Isabella's in-laws, the O'Dempseys, had persistently attacked the town of Kildare. One victim was Thomas Shorthond, who was killed by the O'Dempseys and appears to have been severely mutilated. His body was not found for three days, when labourers noticed crows and dogs gathering in a field. When they went to see what attracted the scavengers, only Thomas Shorthond's head and right foot remained[298].

Nevertheless, Isabella completed her journey to the Slieve Bloom Mountains and returned to the relative safety of colonial territory in County Kildare. Her relief, however, was soon subdued when she and Fynewell were arrested for having 'art and part with ... felons and are spies of the country for them'[299]. It seems that the Anglo-Norman authorities were increasingly suspicious of her husband Diarmait O'Dempsey and his family's activities.

Being accused of aiding the Gaelic Irish in the Slieve Bloom Mountains was a very serious charge; in 1297 Nicolas Toan was hanged after being found guilty of a similar offence[300]. As was clear from several other cases, Isabella's gender provided her with little protection in a conflict in which few were not involved. She was tried, and admitted to bringing gifts from the Gaelic Irish rebels in the Slieve Bloom Mountains to her husband Diarmait. Although she was found guilty and her assets declared forfeit, she was pardoned and avoided the death penalty. The Justiciar claimed that his lax sentence in this specific case was due to what he called the 'simplicity of women in this affair' and 'the praiseworthy service'[301] of Isabella's father. Ultimately, the relations between Isabella's Gaelic in-laws and the Crown reached breaking point, and in 1308 Anglo-Norman forces killed her husband Diarmait O'Dempsey[302].

There were many other men and women for whom the complexity of warfare in later medieval Ireland ensured it was almost impossible to avoid involvement. This warfare was a world apart from the oft-eulogised battlefield of archers and heavy cavalry. There was little distinction between peacetime and wartime in the conflict between the Anglo-Normans and Gaelic Irish, which engulfed later medieval Ireland. In this environment, traditional roles were cast aside in an increasingly bitter struggle that not only took place *between* communities, but also *within* communities as many found their loyalties tested.

## 20

# Sanctuary, Exile or Luck: Evading the Noose

In the autumn of 1331, the Lord of Carbury, William de Bermingham, was in very dangerous predicament. He, together with Maurice Fitzgerald, the Earl of Desmond and Walter de Burgh, a cousin of the Earl of Ulster, were accused of having planned a revolt against the Crown forces. If successful, they proposed to carve Ireland up between them.

The plot was discovered, and many of those implicated were arrested. Walter de Burgh was imprisoned in the remote Northburgh Castle, and starved to death, by his cousin the Earl of Ulster. Maurice Fitzgerald, the Earl of Desmond, was thrown in gaol in Dublin Castle, where he would remain for some time. Last, but not least, was William de Bermingham. He was also imprisoned in Dublin Castle together with his son Walter. While Maurice Fitzgerald would prove too well connected and powerful to execute, William did not have this luxury. As he was only the brother of the deceased Earl of Louth, John de Bermingham, he and his son were more than likely to be executed for treason.

Undaunted, de Bermingham began to focus on the idea of escape, and he devised a daring plan. Having once broken free of his chains, he planned to escape his cell before scaling down the walls of the castle. There he would be met by a small army of 240 men. Unfortunately, the royal authorities got wind of the scheme and raided his cell. There they found not only rope (presumably to descend the castle walls), but also 'devices made by magic'[303] to break the fetters. The city defence was strengthened, and when de Bermingham's little army arrived, it was clear their plan had been uncovered. Retreating, they set fire to houses in an attempt to burn the city suburbs.

Whatever the truth of the original accusation of treason, the arrival of an army, however small, to free him from prison, did little to aid de Bermingham's case. William was tried for attempting to escape, which allowed the prosecutors to avoid a trial on the more difficult treason charges. Predictably, William de Bermingham was found guilty and hanged, while his son, Walter, remained in prison until his death some years later.

This plan to avoid a date with Dublin's hangman was as unrealistic as it was audacious. Bringing hundreds of men to the city was always going to prove difficult, although, to this day, historians are perplexed and somewhat sceptical as to what the so-called 'magical devices' were. While de Bermingham's plan was never going to work, there were others who successfully escaped what seemed a certain death. Many of these escapes were more realistic, if less elaborate and, ultimately, more successful. As we shall see, the medieval legal system contained lots of caveats and loopholes. An astute prisoner, willing to use guile, cunning and violence if needs be, could avoid the noose; others could just be lucky.

Risus de Beket was a far craftier, litigious and successful man, who found himself looking at the wrong end of an execution order in the early fourteenth century. In 1308 he had been convicted of killing Agnes Hore[304], and murder was a hanging offence. Having been apprehended, Risus was thrown into Cork Gaol. The fourteenth-century version of prison was drastically different to the modern institution, however, and security was far more relaxed. While incarcerated, Risus asked the gaoler if he could take a walk through the town of Cork. The gaoler acquiesced, and Risus sauntered out of the prison. Rather than taking immediate flight, Risus adopted a safer option. Walking through Cork, he made his way to the church of St Peter. Once inside, Risus refused to leave, claiming sanctuary. While claiming religious sanctuary stopped his immediate rearrest, he could not stay in the church forever. Under law and custom, he could stay there for forty days free from molestation, but after this his protection would expire. While it would be an offence to storm the church, the authorities could simply starve Risus, which would eventually lead to his capitulation.

There was, however, one loophole, the great medieval 'get out of gaol free' card: abjuration. When two coroners, Stephen Longfeld and John Auel, were sent to ask Risus to leave the church, he refused and informed them that he wished to abjure himself[305]. This was, in effect, a process by which an accused man exiled himself from the realm. In a completely legal procedure, the coroners would appoint the abjurer a port, to which he had to go directly – he was not even allowed to leave the road. In Risus' case, he did not have far to travel, as the nearby harbour of Cork was chosen. Before he left the church, he was given a cross to mark him out as being under church protection so that Agnes Hore's family could not seek retribution[306]. Arriving at Cork harbour, Risus had forty days to secure a passage on a ship. The only one catch in the process was that an abjurer like Risus could only return on pain of death.

While he had escaped Cork prison and the hangman's noose, Risus, like most who abjured themselves, had no intention of going into exile; he had simply bought himself time. In the following years he remained in Ireland, and was involved in multiple crimes. This was a dangerous life, particularly in Risus' case. If he were apprehended, an almost certain execution lay ahead of him. He had only one option: a Royal Pardon. In the early fourteenth century, these were far easier to get than we might imagine. Appearing before the Justiciar's Court on 31 July 1312, Risus received a Royal Pardon for all crimes, including his abjuration and his declaration as an outlaw.[307]

Five years later, in November 1317, Risus found himself hauled before the courts for burning a house and stealing cattle in Kildare[308]. He simply produced his pardon and invalidated the charge. Unfortunately for him, it appears that those prosecuting the case in 1317 held a grudge against Risus, which is hardly surprising given his many crimes. It was claimed that, while he had been pardoned for his escape, he had never been pardoned for his own declared abjuration.[309] Although this was untrue, it appears that Risus was willing to pay the fine in this case. This was unquestionably the best outcome, given that he had committed several crimes, any of which could have resulted in his execution.

While people like Risus used guile and intelligence to avoid the noose, there were some who depended on pure luck. Two such individuals would produce one of the most unusual stories in medieval Irish history.

In the early fourteenth century, the ports of the Anglo-Norman colony of Ireland were its lifeblood. Through its busiest docks at New Ross, Waterford, Drogheda and

Cork, the Norman colony exported large quantities of food, while imports included everything from rare goods to military support for the colonists. Although it was the largest settlement in Ireland, Dublin was only the fifth largest port. However, it was strategically very important due to its geographical proximity to Wales and England. While these ports were crucial to colonial life, they also imported quite a lot of problems in the form of rowdy sailors who worked the vessels. Such was these sailors' reputation for causing trouble that the 1326 Parliament enacted legislation empowering bailiffs to take sureties from sailors to bind them to the law while in port.[310] It was found necessary to ensure the sailors' good behaviour following outrages such as the atrocious murder of one Robert Thurstayn in the summer of 1311.

Thomas le Whyte, himself a sailor, wanted to rid himself of an enemy. It did not take le Whyte long to find willing accomplices for the murder he was planning among his fellow mariners. Five sailors from various ports around England, including Robert Godard of Sandwich and Richard Faber of Lyverpol (Liverpool), were more than willing to get involved. The target, Robert Thurstayn, didn't stand much of a chance when he was set upon. Le Whyte, aided by the 'forcible assistance' of the five ruffians, murdered the unfortunate Thurstayn.

Murder in medieval Dublin was by no means unusual; the sailors probably had little idea, however, whom they had just killed. Robert Thurstayn was not just another random death in the city. Not only was he a merchant, but he had also been a royal official. Indeed, this may have been the reason why le Whyte wanted him killed. The previous year Thurstayn had been working as a royal purveyor, purchasing supplies for the king's armies at war in Wicklow.[311] While the exact cause of le Whyte's enmity does not survive,

Thurstayn's very employment may well have been the source of the tension. Purveyors often sequestered ships to transport goods and then failed to pay up. Corruption and embezzlement were by no means unusual. Indeed, three years later, in 1314, accounts of £54 7s 1d were still outstanding from his fellow purveyors, Robert le Woder and William de Callan.[312] If the purveyors had stolen the money, it is very possible that people like the mariner Thomas le Whyte would have been left out of pocket.

Whatever the reason, Robert Thurstayn was assassinated in Dublin in 1311, and very quickly the authorities arrested the five sailors, together with another man, William le Rede. Thomas le Whyte fled the city to Scotland to seek a pardon from the king, which he successfully attained in July[313]. However, this left his accomplices to face the Dublin courts on their own, having murdered a prominent resident of the city. Worse still, they were penniless strangers – there would be no consequence to executing such men. Had they been wealthy they may have had some chance, but when the jury was assembled, the verdict was not in doubt. There was little chance of their surviving, given that they were facing a jury comprising members of Dublin's merchant families, including Robert le Woder, who had worked with Thursteyn. Naturally, all five sailors were sentenced to death by hanging. The sixth person, William le Rede, was acquitted. He may have been spared by the fact that he was a Dubliner (at least, a man of the same name was murdered in the city in 1318)[314].

The sailors' final journey was one to the gallows in medieval Dublin. After their arrival at the gallows, the five sailors were unceremoniously hanged and their corpses put into a cart, which was taken to Kilmainham Gaol for burial. Upon their arrival in Kilmainham, however, two of those hanged – Robert Godard of Sandwich and

Richard Faber of Liverpool, awoke to find themselves not en route to the afterlife but still alive. How they survived was neither explained nor questioned in the fourteenth-century records. Certainly, the hangman appears to have been above suspicion of involvement. He was clearly able to carry out his duties, given that the other three were successfully dispatched.

Unfortunately for Faber and Godard, emerging with their necks intact did not mean they had escaped the death sentence. Having survived the gallows once, they did not fancy giving the hangman another attempt at successfully completing the job. Once they had found their bearings, the two sought sanctuary in a nearby church, no doubt hoping to abjure themselves. However, the two men were saved not by exile but by another less likely source.

In the Justiciar's court, John of Argyle, the commander of King Edward II's fleet in the Irish Sea, testified for the Lazarus-like sailors, arguing that they were 'valiant and good strong mariners'[315]. No doubt Argyle could use every pair of hands he could find. In the same year, Robert Bruce was increasingly expanding into the Irish Sea, and by 1313 he would conquer the Isle of Man, threatening to cut the sea route between England and Ireland. A sailor's life, while dangerous, nonetheless offered the two men escape from Dublin, where they seemed to have no future at all.

While the case of Godard and Faber was perhaps the most unusual, there were many more who took the simpler route through abjuration, or the more risky strategy of escaping and facing the dangers of life as an outlaw. Nevertheless, as we have seen, in medieval Ireland, a death sentence didn't always mean the end of the line.

## 21

# Trouble on the Home Front: Dublin 1304

In the high summer of 1303, Richard de Burgh, Earl of Ulster and Lord of Connacht, held a ceremony in Dublin Castle. There he bestowed knighthoods on thirty-three of his followers in preparation for a great military expedition de Burgh was leading to Scotland, where he would join King Edward I in his ongoing war[316]. While de Burgh knighted his allies, frantic preparations for his disembarkation were underway in the streets and lanes of Dublin. These meticulous plans had preoccupied the lives of many in the city and the surrounding countryside over the previous weeks and months.

As part of these preparations, a huge fleet of some 176 ships had been assembled from across Britain and Ireland to carry de Burgh's army across the Irish Sea, but before they could set sail this armada had to be fitted out for its military cargo. This saw a large-scale operation scour the Dublin region as far south as Newcastle in Wicklow for saplings.[317] After being transported to the priory of All Hallows at Dublin, the saplings were woven together to make cages.[318] Once transported to the ships, these cages housed the great warhorses as the fleet crossed the Irish Sea. While this work gave employment in the summer of 1303, the costs of the ongoing war between England and Scotland were devastating the Anglo-Norman colony in Ireland. Within the year this war caused chaos, not just in Scotland, but in the streets of the Irish ports.

## The Costs of War

Having safely crossed to Scotland in July, Richard de Burgh joined the forces of King Edward I. Edward hoped that this campaign would be the 'final and happy expedition of the war in Scotland'[319]. Ending what had been a costly conflict would have been widely welcomed in Anglo-Norman Ireland, as the financial burden placed on the colonists by the war was not sustainable. Having dragged on for nearly a decade, the enormous bill had not been footed solely by the Crown. The colony in Ireland had been drained of money as it was used as a key supply base. Tonnes of grains, salted fish, wines and other supplies were shipped across the Irish Sea, where they were landed on the shores of northern England at the port of Skinburness on the Scottish border.

The burden of this was at times staggering. In 1298 alone, £4,000 of the £5,671[320] collected by the Irish exchequer had been spent on purchasing supplies for Edward's armies in Scotland. These costs continued to mount in the early fourteenth century. In 1303, Edward I was so desperate to ensure the participation of Richard de Burgh in the campaign that he agreed to waive a debt of over £11,000 the earl owed the Irish exchequer.[321]

While many of the contingents from Ireland returned home in September, Edward I and the Earl of Ulster remained in Scotland until the following year of 1304.

Supplying this army would prove difficult, and soon further demands were made on the already stretched colonial economy in Ireland. Edward sent messengers demanding that supplies be sent to feed the host now besieging Stirling Castle.

## Trouble at Home

In Ireland, the population cared little about the wars overseas. Merchants in particular were growing tired and increasingly restless about the seemingly never-ending burden of Edward's attempt to conquer Scotland. These demands for increased supplies proved to be the final straw.

The key issue in Ireland was not just the amount of money spent, but also the chaotic and corrupt process by which corn and other supplies were sourced by the army. Royal armies were supplied by a haphazard system known as purveyance, which saw officials, who were given extraordinary powers, sourcing supplies. These officials, known as purveyors, could not be refused by merchants when they arrived in markets. They effectively confiscated whatever materials they wanted, and while they were supposed to pay market rates it appears that they rarely did. Unsurprisingly, purveyors were despised by merchants. Frequently, the purveyors left what were effectively royal IOUs with the merchants when they did not have enough coin to pay for the goods they took. These debts were sometimes paid years later, if at all.

Outright corruption further enraged merchants. In 1307, Walter Reyth admitted to having done exactly this when he had secured a contract for purveying supplies to the king's armies in Scotland. As purveyor, Walter took wines from Nicolas le Veel, a merchant in Cork. When he had received payment for the wines from the king, he had held back forty shillings that was owed to Nicolas for his own use.[322]

Cases such as this led to the view that the system of purveyance was unfair, and all evidence indicates that it was. Even high officials abused the system. In 1326, the former Treasurer of Ireland, Walter de Islip, was accused of buying corn from his friends at a high price when it was available at a lower price elsewhere.[323]

Long before Edward's officials arrived in Dublin in 1304 demanding more supplies, resistance to purveyance had been mounting in Ireland. In 1297, the bishops Robert of Cork and Nicolas of Cloyne were caught, not only hiding food from purveyors, but also threatening the officials with excommunication if they took their crops![324] Such resistance was punished, and even powerful figures like these bishops were heavily fined. Incidents like this were indicative of tensions simmering beneath the surface.

Thus, when purveyors arrived in Ireland in 1304 to supply Edwards's army in Scotland, they found a society that was increasingly war-weary. The presence of soldiers and sailors had also created tensions. In June 1304, serious trouble broke out in the port town of New Ross when the presence of raucous sailors had escalated tensions with the townspeople. On this occasion, Robert Russell, the mayor, had to come to the aid of townsman Robert Seinde after sailors had attacked him. The disturbance, which saw Seinde wounded, only ended when Russell organised a posse and physically drove the sailors back to their ships.[325] This was not an isolated incident; such conditions were known to cause tensions. Later the following year, when the knight Maurice de Carreu was heading to Scotland with troops, he was attacked while quartered in the Coombe, just a few hundred metres outside the walls of Dublin. Among his attackers were members of prominent merchant families in the city, including Robert le Woder and William de Seriaunt. This group, who killed some of Carreu's soldiers, also included the future mayors of Dublin John le Decer and Richard Lawles.[326] It was obvious that when purveyors attempted to take supplies from these people, trouble would follow.

Sure enough, when purveyors arrived in Dublin, these pre-existing tensions exploded. The unenviable task of overseeing the taking of grains fell to William Wythington, a royal clerk sent to Ireland specifically for the task. When he arrived in Dublin he found that 'certain men enormously disturbed the king's market'[327]. Merchants had taken goods stored in the city and grains en route to the market and hidden them. It was clear that Wythington was facing a well-organised conspiracy to keep the grain hidden in Dublin and prevent him from forcibly taking it.

Faced with this widespread opposition, Wythington approached the then Mayor of Dublin Geoffrey Morton for assistance. Morton himself had worked as a purveyor back in 1296, shipping supplies to Gascony and Wythington, and was no doubt hopeful that he would find an understanding ally. But Morton was first and foremost a merchant of Dublin, who had been elected to his office by other merchants in the city. His experience of purveyance highlighted the worst fears such men had: that they would not be paid. In 1304, Morton was still left out of pocket for his work as a purveyor eight years previously in 1296.[328] Unsurprisingly, Wythington's appeals to Morton fell on deaf ears, and the mayor refused to intervene.

While the merchants of Dublin had very legitimate fears over purveyance, opposing the actions of a royal official had serious consequences. Wythington simply bypassed Morton and appealed to the Council of Ireland, a higher authority. The Council had little truck with Morton's protest, and the mayor was thrown in prison. Worse still, Gilbert de Arden, another royal official, revoked Dublin's liberties, which were in effect special privileges afforded to the citizens of the city.[329] This saw the suspension of the citizens' rights to be ruled by their own elected mayor, and placed them under the rule of royal officials.

While Dublin's liberties were restored not long afterwards by the king, this warning, along with Morton's imprisonment, was a stark lesson to those thinking about opposing the purveyors. Eventually, after widespread opposition, Wythington succeeded in shipping supplies from Dublin and Drogheda, although the amounts were substantially down on previous years.

After these vociferous protests, the issue of purveyance continued to be a major point of contention in Dublin. This is unsurprising as the continued costs of war would nearly bankrupt the Anglo-Norman colony. When Edward II succeeded his father as king in 1307, he acknowledged the economic crisis in Ireland. Shortly after his coronation he noted that the cost of purveyance had so damaged the Irish exchequer that there was not enough money to maintain peace in Ireland.[330] As Edward II went on to acknowledge, this lack of resources was creating huge problems as it was the root cause of an increase in robberies, murders and general lawlessness.[331]

Like most medieval English monarchs, however, Edward II had little overall interest in Ireland, and he soon forgot about the dangers posed by the bankruptcy that faced the Anglo-Norman colony. Even in 1315, as famine threatened Ireland, food shipments were being organised to Scotland. These would only end when the Scots invaded the colony in late May 1315.

While many were war-weary in 1304, they could never have imagined how much the war in Scotland would ultimately cost Anglo-Norman Ireland. When Edward Bruce (brother of the Scottish king) landed in Ireland in May 1315, one of his major goals was to devastate the lands that had sent so many war supplies to support the invasion of his brother's kingdom. Over three years later, Edward Bruce was killed at the Battle of Faughart in 1318, but not before his armies had plundered and burned their way back and forth across the colony several times. It would take Anglo-Norman Ireland decades to recover; arguably it was never the same again.

## 22

# Henry Crystede and Ireland's Earliest Case of Stockholm Syndrome?

By the later fourteenth century, Ireland had endured nearly 100 years of almost constant warfare, primarily between the Gaelic Irish and the Anglo-Norman colonists. While there had been a few major battles – most notably the Battles of Athenry, Faughart and Connor during the Bruce invasion – these were exceptional. Warfare in this period usually took the form of persistent low-level raids by the Gaelic Irish and retaliatory punitive expeditions by the Anglo-Normans. Despite the lack of set-piece battles, this violence was redrawing the map of Ireland. The Anglo-Norman colony was shrinking fast through what was an utterly disastrous fourteenth century. The colonist had endured two catastrophic famines in 1310 and 1315, the Bruce invasion of 1315–18 and then the near-apocalyptic Black Death in 1348.

Unsurprisingly, these events impacted life in every way imaginable. Year by year, raids resulted in settlements being abandoned. A journey through the Vale of Dublin in the mid fourteenth century would have revealed farmlands burned and ruined and a population ravaged by war. While this warfare was slowly but constantly undermining Norman Ireland, it also produced acts of brutality that would stand out in the most horrific of twentieth-century wars. The increasing practice by the Anglo-Norman authorities of paying *capitagium* or head money for Gaelic Irish rebels had macabre consequences: this policy led to the ghoulish practice of decapitating Gaelic Irish rebels captured in battle. In 1316, several hundred Gaelic Irish rebels were defeated in the Upper Barrow valley, after which their heads were brought back to Dublin[332]. Unsurprisingly, rumours of ghosts abounded among those surrounded by such gruesome tokens of war. The ghosts of these particular Gaelic rebels in 1316 supposedly rose from the dead and fought one another.

Warfare could produce even greater levels of depravity. The garrison of Carrickfergus Castle withstood a siege for over a year after the surrounding town fell in the summer of 1315 during the Bruce invasion. Receiving limited supplies, the garrison was eventually starved into submission – but not before they were reduced to eating some of their Scots besiegers, whom they had captured during a parley. It is easy to see the economic impact of this warfare, as the Anglo-Norman economy almost collapsed. The demise of Norman cultural power was also starkly evident. By 1366, a Parliament that gathered in Kilkenny introduced wide-ranging laws to try and reinforce Norman authority; recognising what was an increasing influence in Gaelic cultural practices of all sorts, it prohibited colonists from, amongst other things, speaking Gaelic Irish.[333] Despite examples of the direct impact on colonial territory, economy and culture, it is much more difficult to assess how this warfare, violence and brutality affected the people who lived through it. While we get odd snippets such as the strange ghost stories mentioned above, there must have been far more serious consequences for those who lived through such events. Although most if not all can only have been more desensitised to violence than we are today, many of the violent incidents outlined in the pages of this book must nevertheless have traumatised those who witnessed them.

Were events like the decapitation of Mathew O'Ryan (see chapter 1, p. 21) and the like to happen today, psychologists would undoubtedly assess the impacts, possibly diagnosing witnesses with post-traumatic stress disorder. Medieval society, however, had no such understanding of how the human mind functioned, or was affected by such events. As it was not recognised as a specific problem, no chroniclers attempted to record the direct impact of the violence on people or their interpersonal relationships. One man who lived in Ireland in the later fourteenth century, however, did give an in-depth account of his life to the great medieval historian Jean Froissart. In this account, Henry Crystede unwittingly described a life deeply traumatised by the events he had lived through.

Henry Crystede was an Anglo-Norman colonist who lived in Ireland in the later fourteenth century, a society just emerging from the trauma of the Black Death, in which warfare was also endemic. In 1368, the colonists relayed to the king the troubled state of colonial Ireland, which, even accounting for exaggeration, was dire: 'the king's enemies ride in fashion of war in every part of Ireland slaying robbing, burning, pillaging and destroying monasteries churches castle towns and fortresses'[334]. To merely survive, the Anglo-Normans were fighting to standstill. As Henry Crystede himself would later explain, 'the English have always had war with them in order to keep them down'.[335]

203

In the 1360s, the Earl of Ormond, James Butler, was sent into the Wicklow Mountains with 300 horsemen and 1,000 archers on a mission to keep the Gaelic Irish down. Butler was the one of the two great feudal magnates with large lands close to the mountains; the other being the Maurice Fitzthomas, the fourth Earl of Kildare. For Butler, this mission was yet another attempt to try to prevent the Gaelic Irish in the mountains from extending their influence across the Barrow Valley. Among this large force led by Butler was Henry Crystede. He was a close aide of the earl due to his skills as a horseman.

While Crystede had survived the roulette of death he and contemporaries had endured during the Black Death, his luck ran out during this campaign. The Gaelic Irish set an ambush in the mountains and attacked the earl's army. Fighting broke out as the Anglo-Norman archers returned fire under the hail of javelins raining down on them. Eventually, and unsurprisingly, the earl brought his large force to bear on the situation and succeeded in driving the Gaelic Irish back. Soon, the Normans were in the ascendancy and pursuing their attackers, with Crystede following the earl closely. Unfortunately for Crystede, his horse took fright and bolted through the Gaelic Irish line, far from his earl's retinue. Before Crystede could react, one of the ambushers took control of his horse and then steered him deep into the mountains.

Isolated in the Wicklow Mountains, Crystede faced the prospect of death. There was little chance of rescue given that the earl had no idea where he had gone. Despite the relatively small geographical area the Wicklow Mountains covered, Crystede was in a world apart from the Anglo-Norman colony. While there was much interaction between the Gaelic Irish and the shrinking Norman colony, the Wicklow Mountains were completely beyond the reach of the Norman authorities. Henry Crystede's captivity, however, took an unusual twist. His captor, whom he called Brin Costerec (probably a member of the O'Byrne family), did not execute him but instead held him prisoner.[336]

Deep in the mountains, in Costerec's 'fortified house and town surrounded by woods', Crystede remained captive for seven years. Over the course of his captivity, a strange relationship developed between the captive and captor. While Crystede was not allowed to return home, and his captor took his horse, he lived as part of their family. He even eventually married one of Brin Costerec's daughters, with whom he had two children.

Seven years after Crystede had originally been captured, the latest bout of warfare broke out between the Gaelic Irish and the Normans in Wicklow. The situation had deteriorated so much that the son of King Edward III, Lionel, Duke of Clarence, was sent to try and shore up the collapsing colony. In the ensuing conflict, Crystede's captor Brin Costerec was captured. When taken to the English camp, the Earl of Ormond's retinue recognised the horse that Costerec was riding as Henry Crystede's mount. After interrogating Costerec, they ascertained that Crystede was still alive and well, in captivity in the mountains. Soon, negotiations for his release began. Costerec was initially unwilling. When he was presented with no other alternative, however, he agreed to swap Crystede, his wife and children in return for his own freedom. Finally, after seven years in captivity, Henry Crystede was released. When he returned to the Norman colony, a place he had no doubt assumed he would never see again, his attitude toward his captor can only have surprised some. In later conversations with the historian

Jean Froissart, Crystede spoke very affectionately of the man who had held him in captivity. He even described Costerec as a 'gentleman' and 'a finely built man[337]'. This was completely at odds with his general view of the Gaelic Irish. Despite having lived among them for years, he shared the commonly held, bigoted views of many in Anglo-Norman society. He described the Gaelic Irish as 'dour, uncouth slow-thinking and difficult to get to know'[338]. When it came to the subject of violence, Crystede followed a similar thread. Although he must have known it to be untrue, he went as far as to claim that the Gaelic Irish removed the hearts of defeated enemies and, according to rumours, ate them. Hardly the portrait of a man who was at home in Gaelic society, Crystede nonetheless maintained a positive disposition towards the man who had held him in captivity – Brin Costerec.

Clearly conflicted, while he identified with his captor, he appears to have held wider Gaelic society in disdain. Unsurprisingly, once free, Crystede never returned to Costerec. Indeed, he left Ireland to live in Bristol, England. He only returned once, when asked to conduct negotiations with Gaelic Irish in Dublin on behalf of the Crown, due to his proficiency in Irish.

While the concept of psychology did not exist in the fourteenth century, were Crystede to voice these experiences today he might be diagnosed with Stockholm Syndrome – a phenomenon whereby a captive begins to identify with their captor, particularly if they are treated well. While Henry Crystede's story is unique in that it survives, there were undoubtedly many more who were adversely affected psychologically by their exposure to stressful and violent situations. While the story of Henry Crystede had relatively benign consequences, we can only assume there were far darker results arising from being surrounded by such a violent society. Indeed, one wonders: if we knew more about the other stories in this book, such as those of John Madoc, who brutally killed Mathew O'Ryan, would we find past experiences that shaped their lives and produced such violent activity?

# Endnotes

1   Otway-Ruthven, p. 188.
2   Carlin, M. (2008) '"What say you to a piece of beef and mustard?":The Evolution of Public Dining in Medieval and Tudor London', *Huntington Library Quarterly*,Vol. 71, No. 1, 199–217 (p. 204).
3   Mills, J. (1905) *Calendar of Justiciary Rolls Vol. I, 1295–1303*, PROI, Dublin. p. 427.
4   *Ibid*, p. 334.
5   Sweetman, H. S. (1886) *Calendar of Documents Relating to Ireland, Vol. V, 1302–1307*. Longman, London, p. 153.
6   Wood, H. and Langman, A. E. (1914) *Calendar of Justiciary Rolls Vol. III, 1308–1314*, PROI, Dublin, p. 155.
7   Gwynn, A. (1935) 'The Black Death in Ireland', *An Irish Quarterly Review*,Vol. 24, No. 93, 25–42 (p. 31).
8   Gwynn, A. (1955) 'Armagh and Louth in the Twelfth and Thirteenth Centuries', *Seanchas Ardmhacha: Journal of the Armagh Diocesan Historical Society*, Vol. 1, No. 2, 17–37 (p. 36).
9   Lydon, J. (2003) *Lordship of Ireland in the Middle Ages*, Four Courts Press, Dublin, p. 131.
10  Clyn, J. (2007) *The Annals of Ireland*, Four Courts Press, Dublin, p. 176.
11  *Ibid*, p. 178.
12  *Ibid*, p. 196.
13  Mills, J. (1914) *Calendar of Justiciary Rolls Vol. II, 1305–1307*, PROI, Dublin, p. 104.
14  *Ibid*.
15  *Cal. Jus. Rolls, Vol. II*, p. 250.
16  Connolly, P. (1995) 'Irish Material in the Class of Chancery Warrants Series I (C 81) in the Public Record Office, London', *Analecta Hibernica* No. 36, 137–161 (p. 71).
17  Lydon, J. (1997) 'Ireland in 1297: "At Peace after its Manner"' in Lydon, J. *Law and Disorder in Thirteenth-Century Ireland: The Dublin Parliament of 1297*, Four Courts Press, Dublin, p. 19.

18    Based on the fact he was seneschal of Wexford in 1294.

19    *Cal. Jus. Rolls, Vol. III*, p.160.

20    Meslin was a mixture of several types of grain.

21    *Cal. Jus. Rolls, Vol. I*, pp 148–149.

22    *Cal. Jus. Rolls, Vol. III*, p. 19.

23    O'Byrne, E. (2007) 'The MacMurroughs and the Marches of Leinster 1170–1340' in Doran, L. and Lyttleton, J. (eds) *Lordship in Medieval Ireland: Image and Reality*, Four Courts Press, Dublin. p. 183.

24    *Cal. Jus. Rolls, Vol. III*, p. 19.

25    *Ibid.* p. 142.

26    *Ibid.* p. 27.

27    O'Byrne, 'The MacMurroughs and the Marches of Leinster 1170–1340', p. 183.

28    *Ibid.*

29    *Cal. Jus. Rolls, Vol. III*, p. 237.

30    *Ibid*, p. 200.

31    *Ibid.*

32    Connolly, P. (1998) *Irish Exchequer Payments, 1270–1446*, IMC, Dublin. p. 211.

33    The Exchequer collected £3,477, using the figure supplied in Lydon, J. (1982) 'The Enrolled Account of Alexander Bicknor, Treasurer of Ireland, 1308–14', *Analecta Hibernica*, No. 30, 9–46.

34    For more details see Smith, B. (1999) *Colonisation and Conquest in Medieval Ireland; the English in Louth 1170–1330*, Cambridge University Press, Cambridge, p. 100f.

35    *Cal. Jus. Rolls. Vol. III*, p. 159.

36    *Ibid.*

37    Crooks, Peter (ed.), *A Calendar of Irish Chancery Letters, c. 1244–1509*, Close Roll 8 Edward III, §116 http://chancery.tcd.ie/document/close/8-edward-iii/116 (Accessed 23 April 2013).

38    Parker, C. (1995) '*Paterfamilias* and *Parentela*: The le Poer Lineage in Fourteenth-Century Waterford', PRIA, Vol. 95C, No. 2, 93–117 (p. 103).

39    *Cal. Jus. Rolls, Vol III*, p. 189.

40    *Ibid,* pp 189–190.

41    *Ibid.*

42    *Ibid,* p. 190.

43    *Cal. Jus. Rolls, Vol. II*, p. 397.

44    Curtis, E. (1932) *Calendar of Ormond Deeds Vol. I, 1172–1350*, IMC, Dublin, p. 3.

45    *Cal. Jus. Rolls, Vol. I*, p. 238.

46    Rimmer, J. (1989) 'Carole, Rondeau and Branle in Ireland 1300–1800: Part 1 The Walling of New Ross and Dance: Texts in the Red Book of Ossory', *Dance Research: The Journal of the Society for Dance Research*, Vol. 7, No. 1, 20–46 (p. 45).

47    *Cal. Jus. Rolls, Vol. III*, p. 81.
48    *Ibid.*
49    Clyn, *The Annals of Ireland*, p. 198.
50    *Ibid.*
51    *Ibid.*
52    Brewer, J. S. & Bullen, W. (eds) (1871) *Calendar of Carew Manuscripts (Book of Howth)*, Longman, London, p. 156.
53    Camden, W. (1610) *Annales of Ireland in Hibernia,* Ireland, p. 184.
54    Jones, T. and Ereira, A. (2004) *Medieval Lives*, BBC, London, p. 26.
55    Gwynn, A. (1946) 'Some Unpublished Texts from the Black Book of Christ Church, Dublin', *Analecta Hibernica*, No. 16, 283–337 (p. 296).
56    Kershaw, I. (1973) 'The Great Famine and Agrarian Crisis in England 1315–1322', *Past & Present*, No. 59, 3–50 (p. 11).
57    Camden, W. *Hibernia, Ireland*, p. 184.
58    *Cal. Jus. Rolls. Vol. III* p. 176 (although it is not entirely clear, a similar price is reflected in *Book of Howth* 1310).
59    Slavin, P. 'The Crisis of the Fourteenth Century Reassessed: Between Ecology and Institutions – Evidence from England (1310–1350)', http://eh.net/eha/system/files/Slavin.pdf (Accessed 4 June 2013).
60    *Cal. Jus. Rolls, Vol. III*, p. 162.
61    *Ibid.*
62    *Ibid.*
63    *Ibid*, p. 193.
64    *Ibid*. p. 148.
65    *Cal. Jus. Rolls, Vol. II*, p. 148.
66    *Ibid*, p. 183.
67    *Ibid*, p. 148.
68    *Cal. Jus. Rolls, Vol. III*, p. 148.
69    Brewer and Bullen (eds) *Book of Howth*, p. 126.
70    *Ibid.*
71    *Cal Jus. Rolls, Vol. II*, p. 42.
72    *Ibid*. pp 42–43.
73    Bliss, W. H. (1895) *Calendar of Entries in the Papal Registers Relating to Great Britain and Ireland: Papal Letters, Vol. II 1304–1342*, PRO, London (p. 226).
74    Lydon 'Enrolled Account of Alexander de Bicknor', p. 11.
75    Otway-Ruthven, J. (1993) *A History of Medieval Ireland*, Barnes & Noble, New York, p. 128.
76    Murphy, M. and Potterton, M. (2010) *The Dublin Region in the Middle Ages: Settlement, Land-Use and Economy, Medieval Rural Settlement Project*, Four Courts Press, Dublin, p. 80.
77    Davidson L. S. and Ward J. O. (1993) *The Sorcery Trial of Alice Kyteler (1324) A Contemporary Account together with Related Documents in English Translation with Introduction and Notes,* Centre for Medieval and Early Renaissance Studies, New York, p. 40.

78    Smith, B. (1991) 'The Armagh-Clogher dispute and the "Mellifont Conspiracy": Diocesan Politics and Monastic Reform in Early Thirteenth Century Ireland', *Seanchas Ardmhacha: Journal of the Armagh Diocesan Historical Society*, Vol. 14, No. 2, 26–38 (p. 36).

79    Lydon, J. (1987) 'A Land of War' in Cosgrave, A. (ed) *A New History of Ireland, Vol. II 1169–1541,* Oxford University Press, Oxford, p. 241.

80    Sweetman, H. S. (1881) *Calendar of Documents Relating to Ireland, Vol. IV, 1293–1301,* Longman, London. p. 329.

81    Connolly, P. (2002) 'The Remonstrance of the Irish Princes to Pope John XXII' in Duffy, S. *Robert the Bruce's Irish Wars: The Invasions of Ireland 1306–1329,* Tempus, Stroud, pp183–4.

82    *Cal. Jus. Rolls, Vol. III*, p. 240.

83    *Ibid.*

84    *Ibid.*

85    *Ibid,* p. 285.

86    *Ibid.*

87    *Ibid,* p. 284.

88    Bullough, V. L. et al. (2004) *The Subordinated Sex: A History of Attitudes Toward Women,* University of Georgia Press, Athens, p. 148.

89    Mills, J. (1996) *The Account Roll of the Priory of the Holy Trinity, Dublin, 1337–1346,* Four Courts Press, Dublin, p. 38.

90    Gilbert J. T. (1889) *Calendar of Ancient Records of Dublin. Vol I*, Dollard, Dublin, p. 224.

91    *Ibid.*

92    Davidson and Ward, *The Sorcery Trial of Alice Kyteler,* p. 24.

93    *Cal. Anc. Rec., Vol I,* p. 234.

94    Sweetman, H. S. (1875) *Calendar of Documents Relating to Ireland, Vol. I, 1171–1252,* Longman, London, p. 17.

95    *Cal. Jus. Rolls, Vol. II,* p. 75.

96    *Cal. Doc. Ire. Vol. I,* p. 347.

97    Kenny, G. (2008) 'The Women of County Louth in the Later Medieval Period, 1170–1540', *Journal of the County Louth Archaeological and Historical Society*, Vol. 26, No. 4, 579–594 (p. 592).

98    Berry, H., *Statutes and Ordinances, and Acts of the Parliament of Ireland: King John to Henry V*, PROI, Dublin, p. 267.

99    Connolly, P. (2001) 'The Rise and Fall of Geoffrey Morton, Mayor of Dublin, 1303–1304' in Duffy, S. (ed) *Medieval Dublin II: Proceedings of the Friends of Medieval Dublin Symposium 2000,* Four Courts Press, Dublin, p. 236.

100   *Cal. Jus. Rolls, Vol. II,* pp 32, 246.

101   Best, R. I. and MacNeill, E. (1933) *The Annals of Inisfallen, Reproduced in Facsimile from the Original MS Rawlinson B503,* IMC, Dublin, p. 389 (recorded as the year 1296).

102   Berry, *Statutes and Ordinances,* p. 256.

103    *Ibid*, p. 216.

104    McNeill, C. (1950) *Calendar of Archbishop Alen's Register, c. 1172–1534*, RSAI, Dublin, p. 189.

105    Gwynn, A. (1935) 'The Black Death in Ireland', *Studies: An Irish Studies Review*, Vol. 24, No. 93, 25–42 (p. 104).

106    Aberth, J. (2005) *The Black Death, 1348–1350: The Great Mortality of 1348–1350: A Brief History with Documents*, Bedford/St Martin's, Boston, p. 92.

107    *Ibid*.

108    Berry, *Statutes and Ordinances*, p. 266.

109    *Ibid*.

110    *Cal. Jus. Rolls, Vol. II*, p. 33.

111    *Cal. Anc. Rec. Vol I*, p. 11.

112    Gilbert, J. (1870) *Historic and Municipal Documents of Ireland, 1172–1320*, Longmans, London, p. lxxvi

113    *Cal. Close Rolls Edward II 1313-18*, p. 476.

114    *Cal. Anc. Rec. Vol I*, p. 132.

115    *Ibid*, p. 134.

116    *Ibid*.

117    *Ibid*, p. 132.

118    *Ibid*, p. 154.

119    Campbell, B. M. S. (2008), 'Benchmarking Medieval Economic Development: England, Wales, Scotland, and Ireland, c.1290', *Economic History Review*, Vol. 61, No. 4, 896–945 (p. 918).

120    Mills, J. (1892) 'Accounts of the Earl of Norfolk's Estates in Ireland, 1279-1294', *JRSAI*, Vol. 2, No. 1, 50–62 (p. 56).

121    Otway-Ruthven, J. and Smithwick, A. (1961) *Liber Primus Kilkenniensus*, Kilkenny Journal, Kilkenny. p. 28.

122    Mills, J. (1996) *The Account Roll of the Priory of the Holy Trinity, Dublin, 1337–1346*, Four Courts Press, Dublin, p. 67.

123    *Ibid*, p. 12.

124    *Ibid*, p. 15.

125    *Ibid*, p. 10.

126    *Ibid*, p. 5.

127    Henry, P. L. (1972) 'The Land of Cokaygne Cultures in Contact in Medieval Ireland', *Studia Hibernica*, No. 12, 120–141 (p.120).

128    *Ibid*, p. 130.

129    *Cal. Jus. Rolls, Vol. III*, p. 517.

130    Power, C. (1985/86) 'Diet and Disease: Evidence from the Human Dental Remains in Two Medieval Irish Populations', *The Journal of Irish Archaeology*, Vol. III, 49–53 (p. 51).

131    Gilbert, J. T. (1884) *Chartularies of St Mary's Abbey Vol. II*, Longman, London, p. xiv.

132    Otway-Ruthven, *Ibid*, p.131.

133   *Ibid.*

134   *Cal. Anc. Rec. Vol I*, p. 224.

135   *Ibid.*

136   Otway-Ruthven, *Ibid*, p. 28.

137   Ó Donnabhain, B. (2001) 'A Cut Above: Cranial Surgery in Medieval Dublin' in Duffy, S. (ed) *Medieval Dublin II: Proceedings of the Friends of Medieval Dublin Symposium 2000,* Four Courts Press, Dublin, p. 228.

138   *Ibid*, p. 222.

139   Brewer and Bullen (eds) *Book of Howth,* pp 161–162 (this story is reported in William Camden's Annals. Both are based on the annals of St Mary's Abbey, Dublin.)

140   Walsh, M. (2004) *A History of the Black Death in Ireland,* Tempus, Stroud, p. 46.

141   Power, C. (1994) 'A Demographic Study of Human Skeletal Populations from Historic Munster', *Ulster Journal of Archaeology,* Vol. 57, 95–118 (p. 109).

142   Murphy, E. and Manchester, K. (1998) '"Be Thou Dead to the World": Leprosy in Ireland, Evidence from Armoy, Co. Antrim', *Archaeology Ireland,* Vol. 12, No. 1, 12–14 (p. 13).

143   Aberth, *The Black Death,* p. 41.

144   Gwynn, 'Black Death in Ireland', p. 43.

145   Hennessy, W. M. (1871) *The Annals of Loch Cé: A Chronicle of Irish Affairs from A.D. 1014 to A.D. 1590,* http://www.ucc.ie/celt/published/T100010A/index.html (accessed on 9 May 2013).

146   Lucas, H. S. (1930) 'The European Famine of 1315, 1316 and 1317', *Speculum,* Vol. 5, No. 4, 343–377 (p. 357).

147   Power, 'Human Skeletal Populations from Historic Munster', pp106–107.

148   *Cal. Jus. Rolls, Vol. III,* p. 198.

149   *Cal. Jus. Rolls, Vol. III,* p. 263.

150   Riddle, J. M. and Worth, J. (1992) 'Oral Contraceptives in Ancient and Medieval Times', *American Scientist,* Vol. 80, No. 3, 226–233 (p. 231).

151   National Archives of Ireland, MS Calendar Roll of the Justices Itinerant, 33–34 Edward I (2/448/3), p. 134.

152   Unger, R. W. (1981) *Warships and Cargo Ships in Medieval Europe Technology and Culture,* Vol. 22, No. 2, 233–252 (p. 244).

153   Gilbert, *Chartularies of St Mary's Abbey Vol II,* p. cxxi.

154   Clyn, *Annals of Ireland,* p. 236.

155   *Cal. Jus. Rolls, Vol III.* p. 280.

156   Brewer and Bullen (eds) *Book of Howth,* p. 130.

157   Gilbert, *Chartularies of St Mary's Abbey Vol I,* p. xl.

158   *Cal. Jus. Rolls, Vol. II,* p. 507.

159   *Ibid,* pp 507–508.

160    *Ibid*, pp 122–23.

161    Connolly, P. (1987) 'Irish Material in the Class of Ancient Petitions (SC8) in the Public Record Office, London', *Analecta Hibernica*, No. 34, 1–106 (p. 92).

162    National Archives of Ireland k/b 2/9 (2/448/2) p. 48.

163    Phillips, J. R. S. (1981) 'John de Hothum' in Lydon, J. *England and Ireland in the Later Middle Ages: Essays in Honour of Jocelyn Otway-Ruthven,* Irish Academic Press, Dublin, p. 68.

164    Clarke, H. (2003) *The Four Parts of the City: High Life and Low Life in the Suburbs of Medieval Dublin,* Dublin City Library, Dublin, p. 6.

165    Lydon, 'Ireland in 1297', p. 23.

166    Connolly, P. 'The Rise and Fall of Geoffrey Morton', p. 234.

167    *Cal. Jus. Rolls, Vol. II.* p. 22.

168    *Ibid*, p. 167.

169    *Ibid*, p. 246.

170    Murphy, M. and Potterton, M. (2010) *The Dublin Region in the Middle Ages: Settlement, Land Use and Economy,* Four Courts Press, Dublin, p.107.

171    *Ibid*.

172    Connolly, 'Irish Material in the Class of Ancient Petitions', p. 36.

173    *Cal Pat Rolls Ed. III Vol I* 1327–1330, p. 128.

174    *Cal. Anc. Rec.,* p. 121.

175    Davidson and Ward, *The Sorcery Trial of Alice Kyteler,* p. 47 (he is referred to as William Doucemann).

176    CIRCLE, Close Roll 17 Edward III, §45, http://chancery.tcd.ie/ document/close/17-edward-iii/45 (accessed on 3 May 2013).

177    National Archives of Ireland KB 2/12, p. 84.

178    Butler, R. (ed) (1842) *Annales Hiberniae by James Grace of Kilkenny,* Irish Archaeological Society, Dublin, p. 87.

179    National Archives of Ireland k/b 2/12 (2/448/2), p. 84.

180    *Ibid*.

181    Byrne, N. (2007) *The Irish Crusade: A History of the Knights Hospitallar, Knights Templar and the Knights of Malta in South East Ireland,* Linden, Dublin, p. 64.

182    MacIvor, D. (1960/61) 'The Knights Templars in County Louth', *Seanchas Ardmhacha: Journal of the Armagh Diocesan Historical Society,* Vol. 4, No. 1, 72–91 (p. 73).

183    Byrne, *The Irish Crusade,* p. 101.

184    *Ibid*, p. 100.

185    Neary, A. (1983) 'The Origins and Character of the Kilkenny Witchcraft Case of 1324', *PRIA,* Vol. 83C, 333–350 (p. 335).

186    Although it is sometimes suggested (perhaps most famously by Dan Brown in *The Da Vinci Code*) that this was the origin of the 'unluckiness' of Friday the thirteenth, there is no basis for this. The idea appears to have originated in the nineteenth century.

187    Byrne, *The Irish Crusade,* p. 209.

188    Connolly, 'Irish Material in the Class of Ancient Petitions', p. 52.

189    *Cal. Pat. Rolls. Edward I, vol. 1, 1272–1281,* p. 223.

190    Egan, P. M. (1895) 'The Keteller Monument, Kilkenny', *JRSAI,* Vol. 5, No. 1, 72–78 (p. 73).

191    Davidson and Ward, *The Sorcery Trial of Alice Kyteler,* p. 85.

192    *Cal. Jus. Rolls, Vol. II,* pp 335–336.

193    Neary, 'Kilkenny Witchcraft Case of 1324', p. 338.

194    Davidson and Ward, *The Sorcery Trial of Alice Kyteler,* p. 74.

195    *Ibid.* p.29.

196    Williams, B. (1994) 'The Sorcery Trial of Alice Kyteler', *History Ireland,* Vol. 2, No. 4, 20–24 (p. 22).

197    Neary, *Origins and character of the Kilkenny Witchcraft case of 1324,* p. 344.

198    Ward, *The Sorcery Trial of Alice Kyteler (1324) A contemporary account,* p. 26.

199    *Ibid,* p. 53.

200    O'Byrne, E. (2003) *War, Politics and the Irish of Leinster 1156–1606,* Four Courts Press, Dublin, p. 67.

201    Clyn, *Annals of Ireland,* p. 206.

202    *Ibid,* p. 180.

203    NAI KB 2/7 pp. 26–27.

204    O'Byrne, *War, Politics and the Irish of Leinster,* p. 17.

205    Scott, A. B. and Martin F. X. (eds.) (1978) *Expugnatio Hibernia: The Conquest of Ireland by Giraldus Cambrensis,* Royal Irish Academy, Dublin, p. 147.

206    Martin, F. X. (1987) 'Allies and overlord, 1169–1172' in Cosgrave, A. (ed) *A New History of Ireland, Vol. II 1169–1541,* Oxford University Press, Oxford, p. 93.

207    Simms, K. (2000) *From Kings to Warlords: The Changing Political Structure of Gaelic Ireland in the Later Middle Ages,* Boydell & Brewer, Rochester, p. 28.

208    *Ibid,* p. 27.

209    Watt, J. (1956) 'Negotiations between Edward II and John XXII concerning Ireland', *Irish Historical Studies,* Vol. 10, No. 37, 1–20 (p. 7).

210    *Ibid,* p.15

211    Callan, M. (2013) 'The Case of the Incorrigible Canon: Dublin's First Heresy Conviction, 1310, and the Rivalry between its Cathedral Chapters', *PRIA,* Vol. 113C, 1–29 (p. 4).

212    *Ibid,* p. 5.

213    Phillips, J. R. S. (1979) 'Documents on the Early Stages of the Bruce Invasion of Ireland, 1315–1316', *PRIA,* Vol. 79C, 247–270 (p. 259).

214    *Ibid,* p. 260.

215    Connolly, P. (1997) 'The Enactments of the 1297 Parliament' in Lydon, J. *Law and Disorder in Thirteenth-Century Ireland: the Dublin Parliament of 1297,* Four Courts Press, Dublin, pp 158–159.

216 *Cal. Jus. Rolls, Vol. III*, p. 154.

217 Phillips, J. R. S. (2002) 'Edward II and Ireland (in Fact and in Fiction)', *Irish Historical Studies*, Vol. 33, No. 129, 1–18 (p. 9).

218 Murphy and Potterton, *The Dublin Region in the Middle Ages*, p.474.

219 Sweetman, H. S. (1879) *Calendar of Documents Relating to Ireland, Vol III, 1285–1292*. Longman, London, p. 153.

220 Gwynn, A. (1935) 'Archbishop Fitzralph and George of Hungary', *Studies: An Irish Quarterly Review*, Vol. 24, No. 96, 558–572 (p. 565).

221 Gwynn, A. (1933) 'Richard Fitzralph at Avignon', *Studies: An Irish Quarterly Review*, Vol. 22, No. 88, 591–607 (p. 604).

222 Dunne, M. (2004) 'Richard Fitzralph of Dundalk (c. 1300–1360) and the New World', *Archivium Hibernicum*, Vol. 58, 243–258 (p. 244).

223 http://www.ucd.ie/cai/classics-ireland/2003/murphy.html (Accessed on 4 April 2013).

224 Phillips, J. R. S. (1988) *The Medieval Expansion of Europe*, Oxford University Press, Oxford, p. 86.

225 Yule, H. (2002) *The Travels of Friar Odoric*, Eerdmans, Michigan, p. 15.

226 Butler, *Grace's Annals*, p. 52.

227 Sweetman, H. S. (1877) *Calendar of Documents Relating to Ireland, Vol II, 1252–1284*. Longman, London, p. 160.

228 *Cal. Jus. Rolls, Vol. III*, p. 244.

229 *Ibid*, p. 103.

230 *Ibid*.

231 Down, K. (1987) 'Colonial Society and Economy' in Cosgrave, A. (ed) *A New History of Ireland, Vol. II 1169–1541*, Oxford University Press, Oxford, p. 463.

232 Camden, *Hibernia, Ireland*, p.187.

233 *Ibid*.

234 Berry, *Statutes and Ordinances*, p. 439.

235 Watt, J. A. (1987) 'The Anglo-Irish Colony under Strain, 1327–99' in Cosgrave, A. (ed) *A New History of Ireland, Vol. II 1169–1541*, Oxford University Press, Oxford, p. 389.

236 *Cal. Jus. Rolls, Vol. III*, p. 187.

237 Kelly, M. (2001) *A History of the Black Death in Ireland*, Tempus, Stroud, p. 55.

238 *Cal. Jus. Rolls, Vol. I*, p. 348.

239 *Cal. Jus. Rolls, Vol. III*, p. 171.

240 Mills, *The Account Roll of the Priory of the Holy Trinity*, p. xxvi.

241 *Ibid*, p. xxix.

242 *Ibid*, p. xxxiii.

243 Clyn, *The Annals of Ireland*, p. 56.

244 Williams, B. (1993) 'The Annals of Friar John Clyn: Provenance and Bias', *Archivium Hibernicum*, Vol. 47, 65–77 (p. 66).

245 Cotter, F. (1994) *The Friars Minor in Ireland from their Arrival to 1400*, Franciscan Institute Publications, New York, p. 65.
246 Clyn, *The Annals of Ireland*, p. 37.
247 *Ibid*, p. 246.
248 *Ibid*.
249 Cotter, *The Friars Minor in Ireland*, p. 28.
250 *Ibid*.
251 Curtis (ed), *Cal. Ormond Deeds, Vol. I*, No. 808.
252 Kelly, *A History of the Black Death in Ireland*, p. 35.
253 Clyn, *The Annals of Ireland*, p. 250.
254 Boccaccio, G. (2004) *The Decameron*, Wordsworth, Hertfordshire, pp. 7–9.
255 *Ibid*, p. 8.
256 *Ibid*, p. 8.
257 Clyn, *The Annals of Ireland*, p.188.
258 Curtis, *Cal. Ormond Deeds, Vol. I*, Nos 598, 600, 637, 648, 649, 653, 660, 661, 673, 684 and 690.
259 *Ibid*, No. 812.
260 *Ibid*, No. 817.
261 John Bradley estimates the population of Kilkenny at 2,200–4,000 people in the post-plague fifteenth century. Bradley, J. (1999) 'Rural boroughs in medieval Ireland: nucleated or dispersed settlements', in Klapste, J. (ed) *Ruralia III*, Institute of Archaeology, Prague.
262 Clyn, *The Annals of Ireland*, p. 252.
263 Curtis, *Cal. Ormond Deeds, Vol II*, Nos 22, 34, 35, 36, 38 and 48.
264 Kelly, *Black Death in Ireland*, p. 52.
265 Gwynn, 'The Black Death in Ireland', p. 34.
266 Clyn, *The Annals of Ireland*, p. 252.
267 Berry, H. F. (1915) 'Some Ancient Deeds of the Parish of St. Werburgh, Dublin, 1243–1676', *JRSAI*, Vol. 5, No. 1, 32–44 (p. 32).
268 *Cal. Anc. Rec.*, p. 221.
269 Otway-Ruthven *Liber Primus Kilkenniensis*, p. 12.
270 *Ibid*, p. 36.
271 *Ibid*, p. 28.
272 *Cal. Jus. Rolls, Vol. III*, p. 293
273 *Cal. Anc. Rec.*, p. 221
274 Camden, *Hibernia, Ireland*, p. 151.
275 *Ibid*, p. 158.
276 *Ibid*, p. 163.
277 Connolly, 'The Rise and Fall of Geoffrey Morton', p. 242.
278 *Ibid*, p. 247.
279 Clarke, H. B. (1998) '*Urbs et suburbium*: Beyond the Walls of Medieval Dublin' in Manning, C. (ed.), *Dublin and beyond the Pale: Studies in Honour of Patrick Healy*, Wordwell, Dublin, p. 47.

280 Richardson, H. G. and Sayles, G. O. (1961–63) 'Irish Revenue, 1278–1384', *PRIA*, Vol. 62C, 87–100 (p. 99).

281 Clarke, '*Urbs et suburbium*', p.47.

282 McNeill, *Alen's Register*, p. 171.

283 Camden, *Hibernia, Ireland*, p. 188.

284 NAI K/B 2/7 p. 49.

285 NAI K/B 2/7 p. 50.

286 NAI K/B 2/7 p. 50.

287 O'Byrne, *War, Politics and the Irish of Leinster*, p. 66.

288 *Cal. Jus. Rolls, Vol. III*, p. 229.

289 *Ibid*, p. 231.

290 *Ibid*.

291 *Cal. Jus. Rolls, Vol. II*, p. 480.

292 Lydon, J. (1987) 'A Land of War' in Cosgrave, A. (ed.) *A New History of Ireland, Vol. II 1169–1541* Oxford University Press, Oxford, p. 261.

293 *Cal. Jus. Rolls, Vol. I*, p. 190.

294 Hartland, B. (2008) 'Edward I, the Dublin Government and the Liberties of Ireland' in Prestwich, M (ed.) *Liberties and Identities in Later Medieval Britain*, Boydell & Brewer, Rochester, p. 216.

295 Ingamells, R. L. (1992) *The Household Knights of Edward I*, Durham University Thesis, http://etheses.dur.ac.uk/1509/1/ (accessed 7 June 2013).

296 35th Report of the Deputy Keeper of Public Records in Ireland, p. 33.

297 Lydon, J. (1981) 'Edward I, Ireland and Scotland', in Lydon, J. *England and Ireland in the later Middle Ages: essays in honour of Jocelyn Otway-Ruthven*, Irish Academic Press, Dublin, p. 56.

298 *Cal. Jus. Rolls, Vol. I*, p. 176.

299 *Ibid*, p. 368.

300 *Ibid*, p. 176.

301 *Ibid*, p. 368.

302 Butler, *Grace's Annals*, p. 55.

303 Connolly, P. (1994) 'An Attempted Escape from Dublin Castle: The Trial of William and Walter de Bermingham, 1332', *Irish Historical Studies*, Vol. 29, No. 113, 100–108 (p. 102).

304 In some cases the victim is referred to as Roesia, but it appears to be the same person.

305 National Archives of Ireland, kb 2/12 (2/448/2) p. 15.

306 Hunnisett, H. F. (1962) *The Medieval Coroner*, Gaunt Holmes Beach, Florida, p. 48.

307 *Cal. Jus. Rolls, Vol. III*, p. 256.

308 National Archives of Ireland, KB 2/12 (2/448/2) p. 14.

309 *Ibid*, p. 36.

310 Berry, *Statutes and Ordinances*, p. 321.

311   42nd Report of the Deputy Keeper of Public Records in Ireland, p. 32.

312   38th Report of the Deputy Keeper of Public Records in Ireland , p. 55.

313   *Cal. Pat. Rolls. Ed. II 1307–1313*, p. 375.

314   CIRCLE, Patent Roll 11 Edward II, §190, http://chancery.tcd.ie/document/patent/11-edward-ii/190 (accessed 23 April 2013).

315   *Cal. Jus. Rolls, Vol III*, p. 219.

316   Lydon, 'Edward I, Ireland and Scotland', p. 68.

317   *Ibid*, pp 48–49.

318   *Ibid*, p. 48.

319   *Ibid*, p. 42.

320   Duffy, S. (1997) *Ireland in the Middle Ages*, Palgrave Macmillan, Hampshire, p. 132.

321   *Ibid*.

322   *Cal. Jus. Rolls, Vol. II*, p. 383.

323   Connolly, P. (1995) 'List of Irish Entries on the Memoranda Rolls of the English Exchequer, 1307–27', *Analecta Hibernica*, No. 36, 165–218 (p. 213).

324   *Cal. Jus. Rolls, Vol. I*, pp 95–96.

325   *Cal. Jus. Rolls, Vol. II*, p. 106.

326   *Cal. Jus. Rolls, Vol. II* p. 198.

327   Lydon, 'Edward I, Ireland and Scotland', p. 53.

328   Connolly, 'The Rise and Fall of Geoffrey Morton', p. 234.

329   CIRCLE, Close Roll 32 Edward I, http://chancery.tcd,ie/roll/32-Edward-I/close (accessed 6 April 2013).

330   Lydon, J. (1987) 'The Years of Crisis, 1254–1315' in Cosgrave, A. (ed) *A New History of Ireland Vol. II 1169–1541*, Oxford University Press, Oxford, p. 202.

331   *Ibid*.

332   Butler, *Grace's Annals*, p. 73.

333   Berry, *Statutes and Ordinances*, p. 431f.

334   National Archives of Ireland kb 2/7 (2/448/2), p. 52.

335   Froissart, J. (1968) *The Chronicles of Froissart*, Penguin, Baltimore, p. 410.

336   O'Byrne, *War, Politics and the Irish of Leinster, 1156–1606*, p. 2.

337   Froissart, *The Chronicles of Froissart*, p. 41.

338   *Ibid*, pp 409–410.

# Selected Bibliography

Aberth, J. (2005) *The Black Death, 1348–1350: The Great Mortality of 1348–1350; A Brief History with Documents*, Bedford/St Martin's, Boston.

Barry, T. B. (2004) *The Archaeology of Medieval Ireland*, Routledge, London.

Barry, T. B. (1995) *Colony and Frontier in Medieval Ireland: Essays Presented to J. F. Lydon*, Hambledon Press, London.

Berry, H. (1907) *Statutes and Ordinances, and Acts of the Parliament of Ireland: King John to Henry V*, Public Records Office of Ireland, Dublin.

Berry, H. F. (1915) 'Some Ancient Deeds of the Parish of St. Werburgh, Dublin, 1243–1676,' *The Journal of the Royal Society of Antiquaries of Ireland*, Vol. 5, No. 1, 32–44.

Best. R. I. and MacNeill, E. (1933) *The Annals of Inisfallen, Reproduced in Facsimile from the Original MS Rawlinson B503*, Irish Manuscripts Commission, Dublin.

Bliss, W. H. (1895) *Calendar of Entries in the Papal Registers Relating to Great Britain and Ireland: Papal Letters, Vol. II 1304–1342*, Public Records Office, London.

Boccaccio, G. (2004) *The Decameron*, Wordsworth, Hertfordshire.

Brewer, J. S. and Bullen, W. (eds) (1871) *Calendar of Carew Manuscripts (Book of Howth)*, Longman, London.

Bullough, V. L. et al. (2004) *The Subordinated Sex: A History of Attitudes Toward Women*, University of Georgia Press, Athens.

Butler, R. (ed) (1842) *Annales Hiberniae by James Grace of Kilkenny*, Irish Archaeological Society, Dublin.

Byrne, N. (2007) *The Irish Crusade: A History of the Knights Hospitallar, Knights Templar and the Knights of Malta in South East Ireland*, Linden, Dublin.

Callan, M. (2013) 'The Case of the Incorrigible Canon: Dublin's First Heresy Conviction, 1310, and the Rivalry between its Cathedral Chapters', *Proceedings of the Royal Irish Academy*, Vol. 113C, 1–29.

Camden, W. (1610) *Annales of Ireland in Hibernia*, Ireland.

Campbell, B. M. S. (2008), 'Benchmarking Medieval Economic Eevelopment: England, Wales, Scotland, and Ireland, c.1290', *Economic History Review*, Vol. 61, No. 4, 896–945.

Clarke, H. B. (2012) *Medieval Dublin: The Making of a Metropolis*, Irish Academic Press, Dublin.

Clarke, H.B. (2003) *The Four Parts of the City: High Life and Low Life in the Suburbs of Medieval Dublin*, Dublin City Library, Dublin.

Clyn, J. (2007) *The Annals of Ireland*, Four Courts Press, Dublin.

Conlon, P. (1978) *Franciscan Ireland*, Mercier Press, Dublin.

Connolly, P. (1998) *Irish Exchequer Payments, 1270–1446*, Irish Manuscripts Commission, Dublin.

Connolly, P. (1995) 'List of Irish Entries on the Memoranda Rolls of the English Exchequer, 1307–27', *Analecta Hibernica*, No. 36, 165–218.

Connolly, P. (1995) 'Irish Material in the Class of Chancery Warrants Series I (C 81) in the Public Record Office, London', *Analecta Hibernica* No. 36, 137–161.

Connolly, P. (1987) 'Irish Material in the Class of Ancient Petitions (SC8) in the Public Record Office, London', *Analecta Hibernica*, No. 34, 3–106.

Connolly, P. (1984) 'List of Irish Material in the Class of Chancery Files (Recorda) (C.260) P.R.O., London', *Analecta Hibernica*, No. 31, 3–18.

Cosgrave, A. (ed) (1987) *A New History of Ireland, Vol. II 1169–1541*, Oxford University Press, Oxford.

Cotter, F. (1994) *The Friars Minor in Ireland from their arrival to 1400*, St. Bonaventure University, New York.

Curtis, E. (1938) *A History of Medieval Ireland from 1086 to 1513*, Barnes & Noble, New York.

Curtis, E. (1935) 'Rental of the Manor of Lisronagh, 1333, and Notes on 'Betagh' Tenure in Medieval Ireland', *Proceedings of the Royal Irish Academy*, Vol. 43C, 41–76.

Curtis, E. (1932) *Calendar of Ormond Deeds, Vol. I 1172–1350*, Irish Manuscripts Commission, Dublin.

Davidson L. S. and Ward J. O. (1993) *The Sorcery Trial of Alice Kyteler (1324) A Contemporary Account together with Related Documents in English Translation with Introduction and Notes*, Centre for Medieval and Early Renaissance Studies, New York.

De Robeck, N. (1932) 'Blessed Oderico di Pordenone: Missioner and Traveller, 1285–1331', *Studies: An Irish Quarterly Review*, Vol. 21, No. 82, 229–241.

Doran, L. and Lyttleton, J. (eds) (2007) *Lordship in Medieval Ireland: Image and Reality*, Four Courts Press, Dublin.

Duffy, S. (ed.) (2000-2011) *Medieval Dublin: Proceedings of the Friends of Medieval Dublin Symposium 2000 (Volumes I–XIII)*, Four Courts Press, Dublin

Duffy, S. (2002) *Robert the Bruce's Irish Wars: The Invasions of Ireland 1306–1329*, Tempus, Stroud.

Duffy, S. (1997) *Ireland in the Middle Ages*, Gill & Macmillan, Dublin.

Dunne, M. (2004) 'Richard FitzRalph of Dundalk (c. 1300–1360) and the New World', *Archivium Hibernicum*, Vol. 58, 243–258.

Frame, R. (2012) *Colonial Ireland 1169–1369*, Four Courts, Dublin.

Frame, R. (1998) *Ireland and Britain 1170–1450*, Hambledon Press, London

Frame, R. (1982) *English Lordship in Ireland 1318–1361*, Clarendon Press, Oxford.

Frame, R. (1977) 'Power and Society in the Lordship of Ireland 1272–1377', *Past & Present*, No. 76, 3–33.

Frame, R. (1975) 'English Officials and Irish Chiefs in the Fourteenth Century', *The English Historical Review*, Vol. 90, No. 357, 748–777.

Frame, R. (1972) 'The Justiciar and the Murder of the MacMurroughs in 1282', *Irish Historical Studies*, Vol. 18, No. 70, 223–230.

Gilbert J. T. (1889) *Calendar of Ancient Records of Dublin, Vol. I*, Dollard, Dublin.

Gilbert, J. T. (1884), *Chartularies of St. Mary's Abbey, Dublin (2 Volumes)*, Longman, London.

Gilbert, J.T. (1870) *Historic and Municipal Documents of Ireland, 1172–1320*, Longman, London.

Gwynn, A. (1955) 'Armagh and Louth in the Twelfth and Thirteenth Centuries', *Seanchas Ardmhacha: Journal of the Armagh Diocesan Historical Society*, Vol. 1, No. 2, 17–37.

Gwynn, A. (1946) 'Some Unpublished Texts from the Black Book of Christ Church, Dublin', *Analecta Hibernica*, No. 16, 283–337.

Gwynn, A. (1935) 'The Black Death in Ireland', *Studies: An Irish Quarterly Review*, Vol. 24, No. 93, 25–42.

Gwynn, A. (1935) 'Archbishop Fitzralph and George of Hungary', *Studies: An Irish Quarterly Review*, Vol. 24, No. 96, 558–572.

Gwynn, A. (1933) 'Richard Fitzralph at Avignon', *Studies: An Irish Quarterly Review*, Vol. 22, No. 88, 591–607.

Hannigan, K. and Nolan, W. (eds) (1994) *Wicklow: History and Society*, Geography Publications, Dublin.

Henry, P.L. (1972) 'The Land of Cokaygne Cultures in Contact in Medieval Ireland', *Studia Hibernica*, No. 12, 120–141.

Jones, T. and Ereira, A. (2004) *Medieval Lives*, BBC, London.

Kelly, M. (2001) *A History of the Black Death in Ireland*, Tempus, Stroud.

Kenny, G. (2007) *Anglo-Irish and Gaelic Women in Ireland, c.1170–1540*, Four Courts Press, Dublin

Kershaw, I. (1973) 'The Great Famine and Agrarian Crisis in England 1315–1322', *Past & Present*, No. 59, 3–50.

Klapste, J. (ed) (1999) *Ruralia III*, Institute of Archaeology, Prague.

Lawlor, H. (1908) 'A Calendar of the Liber Niger and Liber Albus of Christ Church, Dublin', *Proceedings of the Royal Irish Academy*, Vol. 27C, 1–93.

Lydon, J. (2003) *Lordship of Ireland in the Middle Ages*, Four Courts Press, Dublin.

Lydon, J. (1997) *Law and Disorder in Thirteenth-Century Ireland: The Dublin Parliament of 1297*, Four Courts Press, Dublin.

Lydon, J. (1982) 'The Enrolled Account of Alexander Bicknor, Treasurer of Ireland, 1308–14', *Analecta Hibernica*, No. 30, 9–46.

Lydon J. (1981) *England and Ireland in the later Middle Ages: Essays in Honour of Jocelyn Otway-Ruthven*, Irish Academic Press, Dublin

MacIvor, D. (1960/61) 'The Knights Templars in County Louth', *Seanchas Ardmhacha: Journal of the Armagh Diocesan Historical Society*, Vol. 4, No. 1, 72–91.

Manning, C (ed.) (1998) *Dublin and beyond the Pale: Studies in Honour of Patrick Healy*, Wordwell, Dublin.

McNeill, C. (1950) *Calendar of Archbishop Alen's Register, c. 1172–1534*, Royal Society of Antiquaries of Ireland, Dublin.

Mills, J. (1996) *The Account Roll of the Priory of the Holy Trinity, Dublin, 1337–1346*, Four Courts Press, Dublin.

Mills, J. (1914) *Calendar of Justiciary Rolls Vol. II, 1305–1307*, Public Records Office of Ireland, Dublin.

Mills, J. (1905) *Calendar of Justiciary Rolls, Vol. I 1295–1307*, Public Records Office of Ireland, Dublin.

Mills, J. (1892) 'Accounts of the Earl of Norfolk's Estates in Ireland, 1279–1294', *Journal of the Royal Society of Antiquaries of Ireland*, Vol. 2, No. 1, 50–62.

Murphy, E. and Manchester, K. (1998) '"Be Thou Dead to the World": Leprosy in Ireland, Evidence from Armoy, Co. Antrim', *Archaeology Ireland*, Vol. 12, No. 1, 12–14.

Murphy, M. and O'Connor, K. (2006) 'Castles and Deer Parks in Anglo-Norman Ireland', *The Journal of the American Society of Irish Medieval Studies*, Vol. 1, 53–70.

Murphy M. and Potterton, M. (2010) *The Dublin Region in the Middle Ages: Settlement, Land-use and Economy*, Four Courts Press, Dublin.

Neary, A. (1983) 'The Origins and Character of the Kilkenny Witchcraft Case of 1324', *Proceedings of the Royal Irish Academy*, Vol. 83C, 333–350.

O'Byrne, E. (2003) *War, Politics and the Irish of Leinster 1156–1606*, Four Courts Press Dublin.

Otway-Ruthven, A. J. (1993) *A History of Medieval Ireland*, Barnes & Noble, New York.

Otway-Ruthven, A. J. (1965) 'The Character of Norman Settlement in Ireland', *Historical Studies*, No. 5, 75–84.

Otway-Ruthven, A. J. and Smithwick, A. (1961) *Liber Primus Kilkeniensus*, Kilkenny Journal, Kilkenny.

Parker, C. (1995) '*Paterfamilias* and *Parentela*: The le Poer Lineage in Fourteenth-Century Waterford', *Proceedings of the Royal Irish Academy*, Vol. 95C, No. 2, 93–117.

Phillips, J. R. S. (2002) 'Edward II and Ireland (in Fact and in Fiction)', *Irish Historical Studies*, Vol. 33, No. 129, 1–18.

Phillips, J. R. S. (1988) *The Medieval Expansion of Europe*, Oxford University Press, Oxford.

Phillips, J. R. S. (1979) 'Documents on the Early Stages of the Bruce Invasion of Ireland, 1315–1316', *Proceedings of the Royal Irish Academy*, Vol. 79C, 247–270.

Prestwich, M (ed.) (2008) *Liberties and Identities in Later Medieval Britain*, Boydell & Brewer, Rochester.

Richardson, H. G. and Sayles, G. O. (1961–63) 'Irish Revenue, 1278–1384', *Proceedings of the Royal Irish Academy*, Vol. 62C, 87–100.

Riddle, J. M. and Worth, J. (1992) 'Oral Contraceptives in Ancient and Medieval Times', *American Scientist*, Vol. 80, No. 3, 226–233.

Simms, K. (2000) *From Kings to Warlords: The Changing Political Structure of Gaelic Ireland in the Later Middle Ages*, Boydell & Brewer, Rochester.

Smith, B. (1999) *Colonisation and Conquest in Medieval Ireland: The English in Louth 1170–1330*, Cambridge University Press, Cambridge.

Smith, B. (1991) 'The Armagh-Clogher dispute and the 'Mellifont Conspiracy': Diocesan Politics and Monastic Reform in Early Thirteenth Century Ireland', *Seanchas Ardmhacha: Journal of the Armagh Diocesan Historical Society*, Vol. 14, No.2, 26–38.

Smith, B. (1989) 'The Bruce Invasion and County Louth, 1315–18', *Journal of the County Louth Archaeological and Historical Society*, Vol. 22, 7–15.

Sweetman, H. S. (1875–1886) *Calendar of Documents Relating to Ireland (5 Volumes)*, Longman, London.

Watt, J. A. (1956) 'Negotiations between Edward II and John XXII concerning Ireland', *Irish Historical Studies*, Vol. 10, No. 37, 1–20.

Williams, B. (1993) 'The Annals of Friar John Clyn: Provenance and Bias', *Archivium Hibernicum*, Vol. 47, 65–77.

Williams, B. (1994) 'The Sorcery Trial of Alice Kyteler', *History Ireland*, Vol. 2, No. 4, 20–24.

Wood, H. & Langman, A. E. (1914) *Calendar of Justiciary Rolls Vol. III, 1308–1314*, Public Records Office of Ireland, Dublin.

Yule, H. (2002) *The Travels of Friar Odoric*, Eerdmans, Michigan.

inspire yourself

the sun
is no
less
beautiful
than
the moon
and
you are
no less
beautiful
than them

you
will
come
to
know
your
heart

for it already knows you

you are
so much
more
than you
think

you can
push through
the most difficult
of times
you are made of
diamonds
you are something
unbreakable

never apologise
for being anything
other than yourself

you are your
greatest project
prioritise it

sometimes
it shines
sometimes
it rains
and
sometimes
you are
the same

i cannot fathom
how you can be so damaged
yet despite everything
still find the beauty
in everything around you

instead
of
wanting
to fix
you
find one
who falls
for your
broken
pieces
too

unconditional

you are
a gift
to this
existence

to try
that
is all
you
can do

are you
aware
of just
how
significant
you are?

soon enough
you will bloom

try not to lose yourself
in the fog of insecurities
you will only jeopardise
your own happiness

fall in love
with the
very essence
of your soul

fall in love
with the
entirety
of your being

you are the epitome
of a goddess
and his failure
to see that
does not make
you any less so

never apologise
for being anything
other than yourself

believe in you

not always
will you feel
this way so

loving
yourself
is the
most
essential
tool
that you
will ever
gift to
yourself

make him
regret
the day
he ever
doubted
your
strength

this world
needs you
in more ways
than you
could ever
imagine

a sight
for sore eyes
she was enough
to render you
breathless

move on darling
you are worth more than this

billions
on this
earth
yet
there is
only one
of you

never lose yourself

she
always
knew
that
she was
here
for more

open
your eyes
you have
everything
to live
for

you are stronger than this

never forget
that there
is only one
of you
and you are as
breathtaking
as they
come

learn
to not
let them
phase
you

you
did not
let them
define
you
before

so why now?

the time
you spend
wishing
to be them
spent it
wishing
to be only
yourself

don't
let their
hurt
be your
hurt
too

want it
enough
and
you shall
have it

dreams

live your truth

do not
lose
your own
desires
through
your desire
for them

why is it
you see
the beauty
in all
but yourself?

i

and
to think
you wanted
to end
it all

how can madness be my companion
yet the one who crushes my soul
it speaks to me like an old friend
a friend who knows me
as no one has before
it welcomes me
like one of it's own
i don't know whether to fight it
or even if it should be fought
as it knows me
as no one has before

i may not think or be
like most others
but i am myself
and no illness
will ever change
or taint that

she wore her battles
for all to see
a broken suit of armour

questioning
my worth
that is
something
i cannot
accept
i know
my worth
and it is
your mistake
if you
do not

i underestimate my abilities
to live with no apologies

parts of
my soul
i have
lost
just as
the petals
of the
flower
are lost
when winter
comes
with it's
bitter kiss

wilting

being alone
is not what i mind
but to be lonely
now that
is a different
story entirely

each
scar
is a
story
of how
you
overcame

when the voices in your head
seem more inviting
than those who surround you
now this is the saddest thing

one day i will be free
and i will forever fight
to be so

no one could ever hurt me
more than i do unto myself

belive me
when i say
i will mend
these broken
wings
of mine

even though
this struggle
is like
attempting
to walk
upstream
of the
flowing river
i know
that i will
eventually
beat this
no matter
how much
this current
tries to wash
me away

handle me gently
for i have broken
many times before

frought with anxiety
'i am not enough'
yet she forgot that her just being
was something so enough
even the sun, moon and earth knew it
and they all knew that she would too

i wander endlessly
in hope for an answer
however knowing it lies
somewhere within
my own heart

she drew
you in
like no
other

if only you could buy
happiness
i reckon i would not
have a penny
to spare

pocket change

never again
will i doubt myself
or allow
to be doubted
by that of others

even when
i don't
have much
i know
i still
have poetry

i owe myself
so much more
than i give

i spill these
poisoned thoughts
onto paper
just in the hope
that never again
will they plague
my mind

the love for myself
must come prior
before i can give
that love

she wrote
and wrote
in the hope
that she
could write
her way
to her dreams
someday

i wish that i
could convey
to you
how one could be
so hurt in spirit
that a pain is felt
as if a hole is being torn
through your every being

not one scar less
would make you
any more beautiful
than you already are

time and time again
you have picked yourself up
so trust me when i say
you can and will do it
time and time again

i am blessed
yet cursed
by a mind
which travels
so deep

my skin
is the only
way
in which
i can
portray such
feelings
not even words
can even
begin to fathom
such things

you have
made it
this far
my dear

one day i will find clarity
but for now
i shall seek refuge
in the war that is my mind

i will
pour
my all
onto
this page
and
pour
i will
for a
lifetime

if only i loved myself
as much as i loved
the idea of who i wished to be

i seem
to forget
how far
that i
have come
and how
much further
i still
have yet
to go

why is it
you numb
yourself
darling?

look at all that you are missing

05:36am
and the silence
is deafening
yet however not
within my mind

to be told
that the very
essence
of your core
is broken
and may never
be fixed
is a prospect
in which i wish
not to dwell upon
for too long
at all

diagnosis

i will never expect for others
to understand
however only to listen
and to be mindful

my heart
bleeds
onto paper
in the hope
that yours
never will

i am a woman
and that is something
i shall be proud of
till the day i die

a prisoner within my own mind
with all of the awareness
of knowing it is only i
who can be my savior

you
did not
give up
and for
that
i am
thankful

to fight an urge
that releases all the hatred
all the anger
all of the despair
but leaves a reminder
for the rest of your life
i know that most
will not understand
but for me
it is the only way
that can save me

what it is
to dream
when you
had forgotten
how to do so
for so long

your inability
to see my divinity
is no mistake
other than your own

you
tell me
that i am
broken
i tell you
that i am
as i should

it is then
that she
believed
that she
could
have
it all

every slight pin prick
of pain
i will tell you now
i feel that
like i hope no other does

an open wound

i am
a force
to be
reckoned
with
i am
only
but myself

you have
so much
left to give
do stay

i am drawn
and captivated
by things of beauty
perhaps due to
the lack of  beauty
i see within myself

i hurt and wish
for you to tell me
it will always
not be this way so

feel me deeply

and i
became
the poet
that i was
always
meant
to be

one will
cherish
her
if you
do not

look
darling
you've
made it

them

someone will ache for your soul
wait for them

i poured
my soul
into
whatever
we was
now
i am
empty
and you
are not
here

longing

it'd be nice
for someone
to hold me
when i can
no longer
hold myself

engulf
every inch
of me

never allow yourself
to be anything
but worshipped
he should feel blessed
for your eyes to even
have met his

a soul to connect with
is so hard to come by
cherish it when you do

why are those
who are supposed
to love you most
are those who seem
to break you
into something
so irremdiable

my body
is not
your god
given right
how dare
you
even imagine
to think so
let alone
to even act
upon it

is it so wrong
to long for something
that is real

could you
not as easily
leave my heart
just as easily
as you left me

i am so humbled
and grateful
to those
who have not
let me fall
i thank you
and from
the bottom
of my heart
i will never forget
your graciousness
and your patience
i will love you forever

and
then
i met
you

why?

the pain i feel
for what could've been
but it hurts just as much
for what happened
i hope you are pleased
that you have broken me
just a little bit more
than i already
was

you
find them
when they
are needed
most

soul mates

my body
a canvas
which can
only
be painted
with your
touch

why is it
you waste
your time
on one
who does
not see
the true gift
that you are?

it always falls back to you

a soul mate
a friend
i am just glad
the universe
gave me you

you
taught
me
how
to be
more
of
myself

thank you

lie still with me
until the universe
consumes us
forgetting all
that does not matter
and being all that is

you have poured
what little you had left
into something
so unworthy
you are empty
you are defeated

i am
so lucky
and so
privileged
for the people
around me
i owe you
everything

if he cannot see
what pearl
lies before him
and that is his loss
and another's gain

how another
can feel like home
now that i truly miss

i followed my heart
to you

you cannot come to me
with the expectation
to be fixed
for i cannot sew your heart
as only you hold
the needle and thread
to perform such healing

i gave
myself
to you
gladly

i think
we came
from the
same star
you and i

you linger
in my thoughts
and live
through my words

hardly deserving

i wait
to share
my heart
with one
who truly
wants it

no longer do i
anticipate
you

if only there was
someone to hold me
when i can no longer
hold myself

i can barely
tend to my own
flowers dear
and i cannot tend
to yours too
that is something
that you must do

i thought
you cared
and you can say
that you do
but i now know
that this is a lie
and you only see me
as an object
i hope you think
about what you did
and what it is
that you have done
but i am sure
that this will never
kill you
in the same way
that it has
killed me

before now
our souls
have met
i feel
that i am
home

when i
look
to the
stars
i see
only
you

never far
from my thoughts
that is as close
as i get to you now

you only admire
the landscape of my body
if only you would see
there is a whole universe
to be admired
behind that of my eyes

you took my all
i gave you
my everything

your skin upon mine
so warm and comforting
your arms holding me
keeping me safe
and hidden from
the harshness of this world
your hand ever so softly
stroking my cheek
like there was nothing
more fragile and precious
than my gentle self

seduce my mind
then i am all yours

i wrote
about you
today

no other
has done to me
as you have

no one
will do to you
as i did

hold me
if only
for a moment
but throughout
a lifetime

i lay here
engulfed
in the pain
whilst you
are blissfully
unaware
i wonder what
it is like
to take something
away from someone
with such little care
and such little guilt

shower me with your dazzling light
let it pour into my soul
until i am only but a mere fraction
of the person that you are

we was
the sweetest
of poetry
you and i

when all
does not
make sense
you do

lost
in one another's
constellations
i wish never
to be found
again

when you come back
to say that you miss me
i will already have missed you
more than enough

and in
that moment
it was you
and only you

to find inspiration
in that of another living soul
brings back a sense of warmth
one which i have not been touched by
for the longest of times

i am done
with games
i am done
with whatever
this is

heart play

but
for
you
i
will

did i feel
the way
in which
you hoped
me too?

because you felt the way that i had, love

i will
be fine
my dear
now that
you are
here

what ever
could be
more
gladdening
than the
smiles upon
those that
you love?

i was too busy
searching for your soul
that i forgot to search
for mine too

i envy the stars
who get to cherish
your wandering gaze
every single night

we could
be something
beautiful
you know

just tell me
that you want me
in all of the ways
i want you too

i cannot let anybody in
because you have never left

hold me close to your heart
so i can hear
the reason that you are
here with me now

when i think
of you
i ache
just a little

you have all of me

i opened
my heart
when often
it is
impenetrable
if only i
would have
left it
this way so
as for now
i would not
be hurting
so much so

i share with you
a part of me
that i am not
even willing
to share with myself

a shoulder to cry on
is only a fraction
of what you have
been for me

i gave you my all
all for nothing

touch me gently
but just as much
show me
that i am yours

when you close
your eyes
i hope you see
every inch of me
and ache
just a little

wanting

i know
that
we will
be

the
universe
planned
for us
dear

i miss
that feeling
of us

we was
the sweetest
of poetry
you and i

when i saw you
that was when i knew

if only
forever
was
your kiss

consume me
let me forget
all that is
so i can feel
all that we are

and just
like that
we was

you saw
past
my hurt
to see
only me

us

from my soul to yours

i shan't ask for your respect
it should already be present
regardless of the clothes i wear
the company i keep
and the opinions
that i wish to share

equal

to love
that is
our
purpose

we no longer
search for what
ignites our soul
yet only attempting
to forever feed
our ever so
unsatisfied ego

stay humble

and how can
the sickness
of the brain
not be seen
as real sickness
when other parts
of the body
are so?

denial

there is nothing
more empowering
than the powerlessness
of others opinions

feel
blessed
with all
you
already
have

more blessings will follow

we all live for art

we are so strong
and so empowering
to doubt us only shows
your own naivety

women

bare all
your dreams
for that is where
you will find
your heart

how does one
not know of their magic
with the knowledge
of that they are made
of stars?

no other
can complete
one who
already is

we are worth
a life so vibrant
it blinds those
who made our lives
seem so dull

if it is effortless
then it is true

why should we feel foolish
for caring for our fellow women
we are here to help one another
not to dull and diminish one another

we are
all
as much
as all
is we

to be a writer
is to forever live in your past

a willing sacrifice

surround yourself
with those of like minds
they will help to nurture
your intellect and passion
they are an inspiration
and should be cherished dearly

limiting
your art
can only
limit
your soul

if my tenacity
is too much
then too much
i shall let it be

love for
yourself
translates
into love
for all

please do remember
a moment in darkness
is not a lifetime so

we are
not
perfect
yet all
we can
be
is the
best
version
of
ourselves

only welcome honest intent

who
would
ever
have
thought
how
amazing
this all
could
be?

we live
in a world
where the
amount of
material
upon her skin
is of more
significance
than the man
who preys
upon her and
takes more
than just her
dignity and pride

poetry
saves
all whom
it touches

if you
allow yourself
to see the beauty
within others
i promise you that
the beauty
within yourself
will begin
to radiate
ten fold

to all the women
who live unapologetially
and with srength
i admire you

always

we hate to admit it so
but aren't we all
just wanting to be loved?

be mindful
to those around you
who may be suffering
it may not be so apparent
yet your gentleness
may save them

this is it
take this chance

baby girl
just because
the odds
are against us
does not mean
that we cannot
fight for what
it is that we want

if you live
and breathe
for your passion
trust that it
will succeed so

chose life

today
the sun
shines
brighter
and
for this
i am
thankful

we sit and complain
about how we do not
have enough of this and that
forgetting that we most
defintely have enough
we just chose not to see that we do

fragility
is hidden
behind
strength

all is not as it seems

we have
made this all
so complicated
when it really
is all so simple

to love

darling
you did not want
to be undressed
and for that
you need
to be dressed

breathe
her in
like
poetry

a new
dawn
is given
to us
every day

rise with it

love unapologetially

one gesture
of kindness
is all
that it takes
to save
someone

forgive her
for every man
in her life
gave her a reason
to fear them so

true
strength
is not
built on
tooth picks

only on courage

i pity those
who have lost
their compassion
towards others
and only seek
to benefit
themselves

she wore her skin
just as she should
for her and
her alone

it takes
bravery
to fall

your family
is not always
that of blood
but that of those
whom care
and nurture your soul
without the inclination
of being tied
by genes

but who is to say
what real happiness is
or to what extent it exists
but nevertheless
i hope you find it

the heart will wither
when not watered
with the love it needs

you do not need a man
to validate your worth
you are awe-inspiring
remember that

she belongs
only to herself
for herself

why is it
we break
one another
when we
could help
to build
one another?

why be
envious
when you
can be
inspired?

learn from their light

she is one worth reading
she is one you won't
want to ever put down

From My Soul To Yours
First Edition
Copyright © Eleanor Russell 2019

All Rights Reserved
No part of this publication may be reproduced
without written permission from the author.

ISBN 9781916070653